TRILOGY

Trilogy

Trilogy

Passages from Life Stories in the Time of Slavery

Chip Kussmaul

Other books by Chip Kussmaul:
Elysian Place a Family Renovation
2084 The Reawakening
Coming soon: Breakfast at Buddy's

Cover design by M. W. H.

Inquiries can be directed to IndividualistsUnite@gmail.com

Editor: Following are excerpts from three books of the nineteenth century. The lives and experiences of the three are quite different from each other, yet common threads repeat throughout all three works. The books largely explain themselves, but the following is some basic information before we start reading.

I came across these books by sheer happenstance. I don't even remember how I found them, nor any number of others that I have. But these are three of the first books I read as I explored the history of the nineteenth century, as told by the people who lived it. These writers have taught me a lot, as only the people who have lived it can. And while these three people led very different lives and never personally knew each other, their experiences of the time, and with slavery in particular, bind them together.

The passages start with Cornelia (Patricia in the book), then Solomon, and then Comfort Servose, the character name used by Tourgee. They then repeat in sequence. The readings from each author are chronological. But because these stories don't precisely overlap, the time periods between the stories are not chronological. Cornelia's story covers the time both before and after the civil war. Solomon's is entirely before the war. And Tourgee's is primarily after the war.

Some of the terms and some of the sentence structure are archaic, and I have moderately edited for clarity.

Where I feel that additional information or opinion is warranted, I will provide it.

Whatever you thought you knew about the time, I think these works will go a long way towards expanding your view. And by all means, read all three works in their entirety if you get the chance.

Corneila Randolph
Murrel 1851-1931

'The White Castle of Louisiana', 1903, by Cornelia Randolph Murrel, who used the pen name M.R. Ailenroc (Ailenroc is Cornelia, spelled backward). She was one of the eleven children of John and Emily Randolph, who were wealthy plantation owners and owned numerous slaves. In the book, the family surname is Random.

Solomon Northup
1808-1864

'Twelve Years a Slave', 1853 by Solomon Northup. He was a free black man in Saratoga, NY. While it isn't stated, I think he might be biracial, mulatto, which would not be at all uncommon.

Albion Tourgee
1838-1905

'A Fool's Errand', 1879, by Albion Tourgee While the other two books are autobiographies, this is autobiographical. All the events depicted are apparently true, but did not all happen to him. However, the essential story of serving in the civil war and becoming a carpetbagger in the south during reconstruction, is true. Because of his admitted gross misperceptions concerning Reconstruction, he refers to himself as The Fool. He tells the story in the third person.

1

1-- CORNELIA

Editor: Cornelia writes this story of her life many years after the civil war. She lived through it, experiencing live fire during some battles. Like most of her aristocratic class in the South, she thought that slavery had a basis in nature and was not guilt-ridden. On the other hand, she felt that slaves were to be treated with consideration. It is difficult to imagine such a contradiction today, but it was commonplace in the South at the time. These years later, Cornelia is contemplating that contradiction herself. Notice the flowery writing, typical of her class, at that time.

DEDICATION

This book is affectionately and respectfully dedicated to the memory of my honored father, now with his Redeemer; And to all who have his child-like faith and bear his nobility of character.

INTRODUCTION.

This volume was begun long ago, and simply for a pastime; completed [years] later, to commemorate circumstances and situations in which I figured slightly...to relate them in after days to the younger generation with whom I happened to be thrown.

But the voice of my heart has been urging me over and over again to disclose the good which has been hidden so long, since much has been said against a noble and misunderstood people *[i.e. the Southern aristocracy in which she grew up]* --so much so—it will be a relief to dare and open the door, letting whatever is within take its flight, and speak to the world at large. Perhaps, like the proverbial pebble dropped in the ocean, the ripples may widen to eternity, and be of service to some, or if even one, I shall be thankful.

****

In the year of our Lord eighteen hundred and forty-five, Nicodemus, *a son of Ham,* stood in the market at New Orleans to be sold, and also his wife by his side, who clung to him tremblingly for fear she might not be allowed to go with him, might not be sold to the same party.

She was a slight, fragile-looking mulatto, and her face had a sad, sweet expression; gentleness seemed her predominant trait. She was about eighteen.

Nicodemus was a tall, stalwart, dusky fellow with the mien of one born to command. He might have been the son of a chief, so well did he bear himself. His arms were brawny, his chest was broad, his face of a high negro type, with strength written thereon.

There were others in the market awaiting the same ordeal, but Nicodemus and his wife were the most attractive in that pitiful group.

The man who had the most money would get him.

He was valuable; but his wife, would she, of slightly built frame, be allowed to follow the man she loved—the man, gentle as she was, that she ruled?

Ah! that was the question with her. The pensive air, the clinging attitude, was a picture to soften the heart.

A Southern gentleman, a Mr. Random, was looking about for, or had in contemplation, such a negro as Nicodemus. For, while he felt a sympathy for such a condition of life, he well knew that Nicodemus would be as happy with himself as any other owner. After being assured of the soundness of the man he made a mental calculation that the fellow would serve his purpose and that he would give him the place of upper servant, such as was used on every plantation, supervising the other slaves, to lead them, to direct them, to exert a good influence over them.

But the little girl at his side, what could he do with her?

He had too much heart to take the one without the other, once he discerned their relations.

Fate is often unkind, he thought—inscrutable, in fact.

At this moment the wife, either seeing the softening in his face or fearing the fatal words which she felt might come, fell prostrate, clasped Mr. Random around his knees, and turned her gentle face in prayer to him for help.

Her appeal was not unheeded, her effort was not without avail. All were now looking on with interest; other matters were forgotten, and the light which looked from her eyes was sublime, when Mr. Random told her he would let her share her life with Nicodemus. None of the three ever regretted the occurrence, as we shall later learn.

1--SOLOMON

Having been born a freeman and for more than 30 years enjoyed the blessings of liberty in a Free State--and having at the end of that time been kidnapped and sold into slavery where I remained until happily rescued in the month of January 1853 after a bondage of 12 years--It has been suggested that an account of my life and fortunes would not be uninteresting to the public.

Since my return to liberty, I have not failed to perceive the increasing interest throughout the northern states in regard to the subject of slavery. Works of fiction professing to portray its features in their more pleasing as well as more repugnant aspects have been circulated to an extent unprecedented, and as I understand have created a fruitful topic of comment and discussion.

I can speak of slavery only so far as it came under my own observation--only so far as I have known and experienced it in my own person. My object is to give a candid and truthful statement of facts: to repeat this story of my life without exaggeration, leaving it for others to determine whether even the pages of fiction present a picture of more cruel wrong or more severe bondage.

As far back as I have been able to ascertain, my ancestors on the paternal side were slaves in Rhode Island. They belonged to a family by the name of Northup, one of whom moved to the state of New York and settled at Hoosick in Rensselaer county. He brought with him

Mintus Northup, my father. On the death of this gentleman, which must have occurred some 50 years ago, my father became free, having been emancipated by a direction in his will.

Though born a slave, and laboring under the disadvantages to which my unfortunate race is subjected, my father was a man respected for his industry and integrity, as many now living who well remember him are ready to testify. His whole life was passed in the peaceful pursuits of agriculture, never seeking employment in those more menial positions which seem to be especially allotted to the children of Africa. Besides giving us an education surpassing that ordinarily bestowed upon children in our condition, he acquired by his diligence and economy a sufficient property qualification to entitle him to the right of suffrage.

(Editor: suffrage was not universal, even among white men. Generally, a man needed to own land, or have standing in the community as a professional.)

Up to this period, I had been principally engaged with my father in the labours of the farm. The leisure hours allowed me were generally either employed over my books or playing on the violin--an amusement which was the ruling passion of my youth. It has also been the source of consolation in my life, affording pleasure to the simple beings with whom my lot was cast and beguiling my own thoughts, for many hours, from the painful contemplation of my fate.

I had just now passed the period of my minority, having reached the age of 21 years in the month of July previous. Deprived of the advice and assistance of my father, with a wife dependent on me for support I resolved to enter upon a life of industry; and notwithstanding the obstacle of color, and the consciousness of my lowly state, indulged in pleasant dreams of a good time coming, when the possession of some humble habitation with a few surrounding acres, should reward my labors, and bring me the means of happiness and comfort.

From the time of my marriage to this day the love I have borne my wife has been sincere and unabated; and only those who have felt the glowing tenderness a father cherishes for his offspring, can appreciate my affection for the beloved children which have since been born to us. This much I deem appropriate and necessary to say, in order that those who read these pages may comprehend the poignancy of these sufferings I have been doomed to bear.

1—ALBION

It was the 23d of July in his twenty-seventh year. He had been for several days in a very depressed state of mind. nervous and irritable, beset by gloomy forebodings, wakeful, and, when he did sleep. moaning as if in anguish of mind, talking in his sleep, or waking early and crying out, as if in danger or distress. There was nothing in his social or business relations to justify any such state of mind. He was very warmly regarded by the little community in which he was settled.— a leader in its social life, an active member of the church in which he had been reared. And a superintendent of its Sabbath school. He had a good home, unencumbered by mortgage of any sort; a wife, whose energy and activity kept this home in the neatest possible condition, almost, as it seemed without exertion, and certainly without the tyranny of servants. He had an office in the very center of town, where it could not escape the search of the most unwilling or most unobservant seeker. And a (legal) practice which yielded him more than he had any call to spend. All this should have made him the most contented and happy of men.

Yet, in spite of all these comforting surroundings, he had for a considerable time neglected his business to a marked degree, and seemed to have little interest in those things which ought most nearly to have concerned him. For the last few days he seemed to have had no heart or interest in anything save the results of a battle, which was said to have been fought half a thousand miles away, in which neither he nor any one of his clients had an interest which could have been measured by the American unit of money. Yet this young attorney was refusing to eat or drink, because he did not know the results of said battle, or perhaps because he feared that it might not turn out to his notion.

Metta, his young wife, was surprised and alarmed. Never before had there been any sort of trouble in the breast of her spouse, that he did not lighten his heart of at least half its load by at once revealing to her the cause of his annoyance. But this new trouble he had studiously concealed from her. At least he had refrained from a conversation in regard to it, and revealed its existence only by involuntary symptoms. But who could conceal such symptoms from the eye of love? She had seen them, and wept and trembled at the evil they portended.

On the previous day he had come home before the tea-table had been set, —an hour before his usual time. But somehow she had expected that he would do so. She had peeped through the blinds of her little chamber, and seen him coming; so that, as he climbed wearily up the steps, he found her standing on the lower stair in the hall, her lips wreathed in a smile, and her head crowned with roses, as she waited to spring into his arms.

"Oh Metta!" he said in an agonized voice. He clasped her to his breast, but then pushed her away, and looked into her blushing face and into the eyes which were crowding back the tears she was determined should not flow, " Oh Metta, we are beaten.”

" In what case ?" she asked, at once pretending to misunderstand the purport of his words.

He saw the pretty little trick; but he was too sad, and melancholy had taken too firm a hold upon him, to allow him to reward it with a smile.

“Alas !" he sighed, "this can be laughed away no longer. Blood has been shed. Not a few lives, but a thousand, have been lost. Our army has fought at a place called Bull Run, and been terribly defeated."

THERE were no more smiles in the cozy home after that announcement. He had brought with him a newspaper, whose horrible details absorbed his attention, and from which he read aloud to her the distressing details.

Some days elapsed as he contemplated their own little household, one that had been so happy and complete, but which now must be measured against a nation that had gone to war with itself. He was absent from home far more than usual. Meta feared for her home and her marriage. One day, he returned home in an entirely different state. His melancholy seemed to have departed; and he was strangely, unnaturally cheerful and tender to his young wife. He came up the steps with a bound, took her lovingly from the lower stair, where she generally awaited him, and, when he had kissed her a dozen times or so, bore her in his arms to the dining-room, where the tea-table was already spread. Through the whole meal he rattled on of everything except the fearful Shadow which sat opposite, and which he pretended not to see. When the meal was over, he led his wife into the sitting-room ; and taking a seat by the window, over which clambered a rose-tree, some blossoms from which were in her hair, he seated her upon his lap, kissed her again and again, and finally said in tremulous tone,

" Metta, the governor has called for more troops."

There was no response, except that the bowed head upon his breast nestled closer, and there was a sound as of a sob choked down in the white throat.

" Don't you think, Metta, that I— that is we — ought to do something -- for the country? "

Then came a little wailing cry.

" Didn't I pick lint for two whole days, and sew bandages, and roll them; and [a burst of tears] I'm sure I'm willing to do it every day if — if — if it will do any good."

Then the tears flowed in a torrent, and the slender form shook with successive sobs, as if a great deep had been suddenly broken up.

" Oh, I didn't mean that said the Fool. " Don't you think I ought to do something? — that I ought to --go ? "

"Go where?" came the response in assumed wonder; for she refused understand.

"To the war, dear," he answered gently.

"What!," she cried. "You! You! My husband! Oh, it is not, it can not be so! Surely there is no need of that? Oh darling, I should die!"

She sobbed as if about to make good her words, and clung about his neck with kisses and tears mingled in distracted confusion.

" Oh, if I should lose you ! Darling, darling ! think of our pretty home ! Your bright future, and — and," she whispered something in his ear. "Surely some must stay at home; and why not you? "

"Nay, nay, darling," he said, " do not tempt me! I know it is hard; but I could not look you in the face, and know that I had shirked the call. Nay more, my darling ! I could not gaze without a blush into the innocent face of our little child, if I should fail to take a man's part in the great struggle which the nation is waging against the wrong! I could not see your babe, and think that it might some time blush for its father's cowardice!"

The young wife saw that it was useless to argue with a mind so evidently distorted in its apprehension of facts, and lay weeping and sobbing in his arms until he had fired her fancy with bright pictures of military glory and the sweets of the return home, when Peace should crown him with -laurels, and spread a feast of all good things for the heroes who went forth to battle for the right.

So, in a few days, he marched forth clad in the foolish foppery of war, avoiding his wife's tearful gaze, and taking pride and credit to himself for so doing.

2

2—— **CORNEILA**
It was early summer. At a certain point, between the outskirts of a Southern swamp and the banks of the great Mississippi, looking westward from the levee (which flanks the mighty river in the low parts of its flow), broad fields of cultivated land and a growing crop greeted the eye.

A sugar-house, about a mile back, in the center of the plantation, lifted its tall chimneys midst the vast fields of waving blue-green cane, like a ship on the bosom of the sea.

Over the fields and still farther away one caught a dim outline of a low purple fringe of forest which bordered some open ground toward the swamp. A closer look showed it to be a dense copse of wood and tangled vines, where the tall switch-cane made a secure refuge for wild things. And here the adjoining corn-field was called the " Bear-field " because Bruin came out of this convenient lair and destroyed corn every season. In front, on an ample pasture, a flock of sheep were browsing, and numerous cows were quietly ruminating under great live oaks, whose far-reaching branches were draped with that long, gray, hanging moss which lends such unusual charm to Southern landscape.

A bayou through the pasture stole slowly and silently along beneath the summer sun, where the lowing herd were wont to cool their bulky bodies. Thence along, it ran under a fancy wooden fence, which enclosed the grounds around the dwelling place ; cutting off a corner and running to the sugar-fields beyond.

The country was level—not a hill to be seen—except about the dwelling, where inventive man had devised a grotto here, a terrace there ; and picturesque vistas of them appeared through clumps of trees. The grass was a beautiful emerald green, with that indescribable sheen observed only in a clime where grateful vegetation lifts its radiant head to a most genial sun. Across the public road from the foot of the levee a stately gate, with a small one on either side for pedestrians, guarded the carriage approach, which wound at leisure over the front pasture through groups of catalpa, magnolia grandiflora, and other trees, until it reached a green iron carriage gate, dividing a low hawthorn hedge, beyond which it continued its way through a long avenue of Normandy poplars, where, at intervals, stood mythological characters in marble.

When the drive left the poplars it turned around a circle leading to the mansion, and through which a narrow walk rambled an inviting place to stroll and lose one's self beneath the trees and shrubs ; or loll on rustic seats—some formed by growing vines of yellow jasmine—inhaling the delicious odor of the overhanging blossoms, while listening to the mockingbird's sweet notes in imitation of every warbler.

The terrace was formed by what was said to have once been an Indian mound, and rose rather abruptly from the left side of the circle, shelving down to the center of it. There was a narrow walk on the highest part, running east and west, bordered by oleander trees and which dropped down toward the façade of the house and toward the front, near the iron gate, by way of steps. Beneath it was a grotto facing the walk in the circle just mentioned. The whole gave a pretty variety to the front yard.

On the right of the avenue was the greenhouse, and near the turn of the circle on the same side was a fancy shed, used as a shelter for waiting vehicles and saddle-horses. Flower beds sprawled around here wherever it was suitable to have them. In the distance from here was a vista of majestic live oaks and a fence screening the negro quarters, from whence on a still night came the faint turn-turn of the banjo, accompanied often by a rich, sonorous voice of melody, which might have given dignity to a more classic air. On the left, a few paces from the circle, near the house, under shade trees, were the girls' see¬saws ; the boys' playground, partly hid by Japan plum trees and pomegranate bushes ; farther front the school house, where the private teachers held sway. A stone's throw south of these was an orchard of several acres, filled with semi-tropic fruits and nut trees, and stretching on in ample proportions a garden for the plantation family of several hundreds.

The dwelling faced the rising sun ; was a two-story edifice, and with basement and attic ; strongly built and painted white, with an immense portico in front and on the right, upheld by massive columns. Behind the columns iron balconies projected from a second story at convenient intervals, hanging halfway over the spacious gallery below, making a cool nook for those who wished to linger, en negligée, in sultry weather. The front gallery was long and high. The entrance steps leading to it were of gray granite ; there was a pair of them, and they curved around gracefully like those at the palace at Fontainebleau in France, meeting on a projection of the gallery.

A tall, glossy, symmetrical magnolia grandiflora shaded one side of the gallery, its white flowers, as large as one's two hands, giving out a pungent fragrance ; a group of cedars added to the privacy of the other side, neither interfering with the flower-beds which clustered around the walls. An old-fashioned pull-bell, with silver handle, at the right of the door, announced the visitor. Within, the ceiling of the long, carpeted hall was arched and supported by a double row of columns relieved in flower designs at the top ; a stucco wreath formed the frieze ; a mirror in the distance reflected the columns, doubling the length to the observer and giving an Alhambra effect as one crossed the threshold. About the middle of the hall, at the right, was a passage disclosing a broad, mahogany stairway, the steps carpeted with velvet. At the first landing a stained-glass window cast a mellow light above and below, especially at evening, when the sun's slanting rays were melting into the horizon. At this season the window, being semi-open, framed a view of an artificial lake and an artistic summer house on a tiny island in the center. A little boat moored near the edge and two swans floating on the glassy surface completed the picture. From this landing the stairs turned, and continued on their way to a hall in the second story. Here stood two bronze statues of ancient warriors with drawn lances, as if to guard the shadows of the past—the portraits of ancestors on the walls. At the front window was a handsome stand of ferns, and over it a red damask curtain looped on one side, with a heavy cord and tassel. High-backed chairs and mammoth sofas stood erect against the walls, and two queer old tables (drawn to the center) which a Marquise (one of the ancestors) had used broke the stiffness in a measure, through they were staid enough themselves, even while decorated with vases of gracefully arranged flowers.

The Randoms—for such was the family name--took much pride in this hall, calling it the " Hall of their Ancestors," and such it was ; they and some of their belongings were here together. The sword and belt of a grandfather hung beneath his portrait. An old Bible of a grandmother, evincing piety, was on a bracket within her reach ; and about each was some memento he or she had prized in days of auld lang syne. The rooms opening on this hall were bed-chambers—each complete in regard to beauty and the luxury of the day, and was distinguished either by some prevailing color or by the texture of the wood furnishing.

There was a rosewood room,. which the children looked upon with something akin to awe as well as admiration, for only the most distinguished guests ever occupied it, and the superstitious darkies had tales among themselves, that were occasionally over¬heard, about ghosts chasing each other in and out on summer nights. The walls were white all over the house, done in plaster, as smooth as satin ; the frieze, wrought in designs of flowers and arabesque, in stucco ; the woodwork, white enamel finish, with panels of delicate tints. Empress Eugenie held sway in France, and all such things were a la Paris and not a l'Anglaise, as at present.

French ornaments stood on the Italian marble mantels ; exquisite toilet sets graced the tops of the richly carved bureaus, including the dainty puff box of silver or of ivory, holding the most essential element of the toilet. How frivolous, you may say, if you have any prejudice against these fair women but not so, if you saw how cool they seemed a warm summer day, deftly powdered after a refreshing bath ; so masterful the touch, it seemed but the pollen of the flower ; and what a dainty, subtle fragrance pervaded the atmosphere as they gracefully sauntered about.

2--SOLOMON

During the winter I was employed with others repairing the Champlain canal [which connected with the Erie canal], on that section over which William Van Nortwick was superintendent. David McEachron had the immediate charge of the men in whose company I labored. By the time the canal opened in the spring, I was enabled, from the savings of my wages, to purchase a pair of horses, and other things necessarily required in the business of navigation.

Having hired several efficient hands to assist me, I entered into contracts for the transportation of large rafts of lumber from Lake Champlain to Troy [NY]. Dyer Beckwith and Mr. Barthelemy of Whitehall accompanied me on several trips. During the season I became perfectly familiar with the art and mysteries of rafting--a knowledge which afterwards enabled me to render profitable service to a worthy master and to astonish the simple witted lumbermen on the banks of the Bayou Boeuf.

In one of my voyages down Lake Champlain, I was induced to make a visit to Canada. Repairing to Montreal, I visited the cathedral and other places of interest in that city, from whence I continued my excursion to Kingston and other towns, obtaining a knowledge of localities, which was also of service to me afterwards, as will appear towards the close of this narrative. Having completed my contracts on the canal satisfactorily to myself and to my employer, and not wishing to remain idle, now that the navigation of the canal was again suspended, I entered into another contract with Medad Gunn, to cut a large quantity of wood. In this business I was engaged during the winter of 1831-32.

I was in the habit, at Saratoga, of purchasing articles necessary for my family at the stores of Mr. Cephas Parker and Mr. William Perry, gentlemen towards whom, for many acts of kindness, I entertained feelings of strong regard. It was for this reason that, 12 years afterwards, I caused to be directed to them the letter, which is hereafter inserted, in which was the means, in the hands of Mr. Northup, of my fortunate deliverance.

While living at the United States hotel, I frequently met with slaves, who had accompanied their masters from the South. They were always well dressed and well provided for, leading apparently an easy life, with but few of its ordinary troubles to perplex them. Many times they entered into conversation with me on the subject of slavery. Almost uniformly I found they cherished a secret desire for liberty. Some of them expressed the most ardent anxiety to escape, and consulted me on the best method of effecting it. The fear of punishment, however, which they knew was certain to attend their recapture and return, in all cases proved sufficient to deter them from experiment. Having all my life breathed the free air of the North, and conscious that I possessed the same feelings and affections that find a place in the white man's breast; Conscious, moreover, of an intelligence equal to that of some men, at least, with a fairer skin, I was too ignorant, perhaps too independent, to conceive how anyone could be content to live in the abject condition of a slave. I could not comprehend the justice of that law, or that religion, which upholds or recognizes the principle of slavery; And never once, I am proud to say, did I fail to counsel anyone who came to me, to watch for his opportunity, and strike for freedom.

2-- ALBION

Four years have elapsed, (since he marched off to war, now returned home) and our fool is lying on the greensward, under the clustering maples, in front of the little cottage from which he marched away in stoical disregard of his young wife's tears.

It may be said that she has some pardonable pride in the éclat with which he returns. He has been promoted and gazetted for gallant conduct; and general orders and reports have contained his name ; while the newspapers have teemed with glowing accounts of his gallantry. He is a colonel now ; has been brevetted a brigadier-general, but despises the honor which comes as a thing of course, instead of being won by hard knocks. He is over thirty ; and, as he romps with their first-born, his wife looks forward to how many ages of ecstasy in the sweet seclusion of their pretty home.

"There, there, Lily! go and play with your dog," Metta says at length. " You will tire papa. He is not used to having such a sturdy little girl to romp with him."

She is half jealous of the child, with whom she shares her husband's attention which she has hungered for so long. The child goes over to the old Newfoundland who is stretched at ease on the other side of the tree ; and, when the parents look again, her golden curls are spread upon his shaggy coat, and both are asleep. The wife draws her husband's hand upon her knee, lets fall her needle, and forgets the world in the joy of his presence and of communion with him.

" Do you know, Metta," he said after a long silence, " that I have half a mind to go back? "

" Back! where ?", she asked in surprise.

" Why, back to the South, whence I have just come," he answered.

" What! to live ? " she asked, with wide, wondering eyes.

" Certainly: at least I hope so," he responded gayly.

" But you are not in earnest, Comfort, surely," with an undertone of pain in her voice.

" Indeed I am, dear! " he replied. " You see, this is the way I look at it. I have been gone four years. These other fellows, Gobard and

Clarke have come in, and got my practice all away. It could not be otherwise. If not they, it would have been some others. People must have lawyers as well as doctors. So I must start anew, even if I remain here."

"But it will not be difficult," she interrupted. " You do not know how many of your old clients have asked about you, and were only waiting for your return to give you their business again."

" Of course; but it will be slow work, and I have lost four years. Remember, I am over thirty now; and we have only our house and the surplus of my savings in the army, — not anything like the competency I hoped to have secured by this time," he said somewhat gloomily.

"But surely there is no haste. We are yet young, and have only Lily. We can live very snugly, and you will soon have a much better business than ever before. I am sure of that," she hastened to say.

" But, darling, do you know I am half afraid to stay here? It is true I look brown and rugged from exposure, — as who that went to the sea with Sherman does not ? — and my beard, which has grown long and full, no doubt gives me a look of sturdiness and strength; but for several months I have been far from well. I weigh much less than when I left here; and this old wound in my lungs has been troubling me a deal of late. Dr. Burns told me that my only chance for length of days was a long rest in a genial climate. He says I am worn out; and of course it shows at the weak point, just like a chain. I am afraid I shall never practice my profession again. It hardly seems as if I could stand it to sit at the desk, or address a jury.

" Is it so, darling ? " she asked with trembling lips, while the happiness fled out of her face, and left the dull gray which had come to be its accustomed look during those long years of waiting.

" Yes," he answered tenderly; "but do not be alarmed. It is nothing serious, — at least not now. I was thinking, as we had to begin over after a fashion, whether, considering every thing, it would not be best to go South. We could buy a plantation, and settle down to country life for a few years and I may get over all traces of this difficulty in that climate. This is what the doctor advises."

"But will it be safe there ? Can we live there among the rebels ? " she inquired anxiously.

"Oh," he responded promptly, "I have no fear of that! The war is over, and we who have been fighting each other are now the best of friends. I do not think there will be a particle of danger. For a few months there may be disorders in some sections; but they will be very rare, and will not last any time."

" Well, dear," she said thoughtfully, " you know that I will always say as Ruth did, and most cheerfully too, 'Whither thou goest, I will go.' You know better than I; and, if your health demands it, no consideration can be put beside that. Yet I must own that I have serious apprehensions in regard to it."

" Oh," he replied, " there must be great changes, of course! Slavery has been broken up, and things must turn into new grooves; but I think the country will settle up rapidly, now that slavery is out of the way. Manufactures will spring up, immigration will pour in, and it will be just the pleasantest part of the country. I believe one-fifth of our soldiers — and the very best part of them too — will find homes in the South in less than two years, just as soon as they can clear out their old places, and find new ones there to their mind."

So he talked, forgetful of the fact that the social conditions of three hundred years are not to be overthrown in a moment, and that differences which have outlasted generations, and finally ripened into war, are never healed by simple victory, —that the broken link can not be securely joined by mere juxtaposition of the fragments, but must be fused and hammered before its fibers will really unite.

3

3—— CORNELIA

Editor –This house, Nottoway, still exists. My wife and I toured the mansion a few years ago.

From the observatory, a tower approached by a staircase leading from the " Ancestral Hall," a most comprehensive view of the surrounding country was presented. The plantations, with their attendant cottages, gave the impression of a rambling city of vast dimensions. Numerous crafts passed to and fro. [on the Mississippi]

At night some majestic steamboat, plying its busy way, presented a most animated and entrancing sight. Two colored lights, suspended in the darkness from the tall chimneys, appeared to be red and blue stars guiding a great leviathan, whose sides glowed with many colors as the lights flashed along the spacious cabin.

The wheels beat a quick tattoo, churning to a luminous froth the dark bosom of the stream, sending moonbeams, that chase myriads more in glittering train behind. Dark figures flitted around the lower deck in the red glow of the open furnace doors, while above trailed in silhouette against the sky a black cloud of smoke, studded with a million sparks. The throbbing engines—filling the mind with the wonder of their power—forced the delusion of beholding a living thing. The characteristics of the boats varied so that one would know them in the dark unerringly by the sound of steam-pipe or whistle, as you would recognize unseen the step and voice of friends from those of strangers.

The view of the great Mississippi—truly the Father of Waters—from this outlook upon a Southern night was charming to the eye and thrilling to the soul. For the lustrous stars shone above and below in its depths; and the beautiful orb of night at its full, with its quivering rays, cast a glorious sheen upon the hasty ripples of the tortuous stream, wafting the thoughts on toward the mysterious heavens and the great unknown—a fitting place for the children to trace the constellations with their Yankee teachers. You must know that with us everything north of Virginia and Kentucky was called in round terms " Yankee."

Why have Northern teachers ? some may ask, Principally because they made it an object to qualify themselves for this vocation, as in the South the poor relations being usually supported by the richer ones there seemed no necessity for them to fit themselves as teachers; and when the planters sent their daughters and sons N to complete their education it was as much for the change in climate and scenes As for book learning. If the north had observed a similar intercourse, the two sections would have understood each other better. At the White Castle there were at at different times teachers of several nationalities-- a Greek master for music, who came several times a week; a French master for teaching the Terpsichorean art, who came for a month at interval; and an English governess, besides those mentioned above-- all introducing some outside element, which had a tendency to broaden the views and make cosmopolitans of children yet too young to leave the family circle and become so by travel and observation, rubbing off provincialism and making them feel thoroughly conversant with the outside world. There were schools in New Orleans where music and French were easily acquired, as well as beautiful manners, and the young ladies of a family were frequently sent there after being grounded at home in the more solid branches, though I know of one family of lovely woman who were almost entirely educated by the graceful and accomplished wife of Mr. John James Audubon, F. R. S., the great ornithologist. They use generally went to one of the Virginia colleges or to their own State College; Frequently to Europe and sometimes north, after being well instructed at home by tutors.

3—SOLOMON

Author –Solomon, having trusted the wrong people, who had promised him work in the South, has been kidnapped into slavery. Remember, there is no form of communication beyond letter writing and newspapers. Travel is largely by walking and by carriage. There is nothing that Solomon can do to contact friends back home and alert them of his plight. Below, he describes the slave pen in which he finds himself. It is the slave pen of James Burch, who has purchased him for resale.

The light admitted through the open door enabled me to observe the room in which I was confined. It was about 12 feet square-the walls of solid masonry. The floor was of heavy plank. There was one small window, crossed with great iron bars, with an outside shutter, securely fastened.

An iron-bound door led into adjoining cell, or vault, wholly destitute of windows, or any means of admitting light. The furniture of the room in which I was, consisted of the wooden bench on which I sat, an old-fashioned, dirty box stove, and besides these, in either cell, there was neither bed, nor blanket, nor any other thing whatever.

The building, *to which the yard was attached*, was two stories high, fronting on one of the public streets of Washington. Its outside presented only appearance of a quiet private residence. A stranger looking at it, would never have dreamed of its execrable uses. Strange as it may seem, within plain sight of this same house, looking down from its commanding height upon it, was the Capitol. The voices of patriotic representatives boasting of freedom and equality, and the rattling of the poor slaves chains, almost commingled. A slave pen within the very shadow of the Capitol!

Such is a correct description as it was in 1841, of Williams slave pen in Washington, in one of the cellars of which I found myself so unaccountably confined.

"Well, my boy, How do you feel now?" Said Burch, as he entered through the open door. I replied that I was sick, and inquired the cause of my imprisonment. He answered that I was his slave--that he had bought to me, and that he was about to send me to New Orleans. I asserted, aloud and boldly, that I was a free man--a resident of Saratoga, where I had a wife and children, who were also free, and that my name was Northup. I complained bitterly of the strange treatment I had received, and threatened, upon my liberation, to have satisfaction for the wrong. He denied that I was free, and with an emphatic oath, declared that I came from Georgia. Again and again I asserted I was no man's slave, and insisted upon his taking off my chains at once. He endeavored to hush me, as if he feared my voice would be overheard. But I would not be silent, and denounced the authors of my imprisonment, whoever they might be, as unmitigated villains. Finding he could not quiet me, he flew into a towering passion. With blasphemous oath, he called me a black liar, a run away from Georgia, and every other profane and vulgar epithet that the most indecent fancy could conceive.

During this time Radburn, Burch's helper, was standing silently by. His business was to oversee this human, or rather inhuman stable, receiving slaves, feeding and whipping them, at the rate of two shillings a head per day. Turning to him, Burch ordered the paddle and cat-o-nine tails to be brought in. He disappeared and in a few moments returned with these instruments of torture. The paddle, as it is termed in slave-beating parlance, or at least the one with which I first became acquainted, and for which I now speak, was a piece of hard-wood bored, 18 or 20 inches long, molded to the shape of an old fashioned pudding stick, or ordinary oar. The flattened portion, which was about the size and circumference of two open hands, was bored with a small auger in numerous places. The cat was a large rope of many strands unraveled, and a knot tied at the extremity of each.

As soon as these formidable whips appeared, I was seized by both of them, and roughly divested of my clothing. My feet, as has been stated, were fastened to the floor. Drawing me over the bench, face downwards, Redburn placed his heavy foot upon the fetters, between my wrists, holding them painfully to the floor. With the paddle, Burch commenced to beating me. Blow after blow was inflicted upon my naked body. When his unrelenting arm grew tired, he stopped and asked if I still insisted I was a free man. I did insist upon it, and then the blows were renewed, faster and more energetically, if possible, than before. When again tired, he would repeat the same question, and receiving the same answer, continue his cruel labor. All this time, the incarnate devil was uttering most fiendish oaths. At length the paddle broke, leaving the useless handle in his hand. Still I would not yield. All his brutal blows could not force from my lips the foul lie that I was a slave. Casting madly on the floor the handle of the broken paddle, he seized the rope. This was far more painful than the other. I struggled with all my power, but it was in vain. I prayed for mercy, but my prayer was only answered with imprecations and with stripes. I thought I must die before the lashes of the accursed brute. Even now the flesh crawls upon my bones, as I recall the scene. I was all on fire. My sufferings I can compare to nothing else than the burning agonies of hell!

Editor—About two weeks later, Solomon and a group of other slaves are walked from the slave pen to a steamboat, for the trip down river.

Reaching the Steamboat, we were quickly hustled into the hold, among barrels and boxes of freight. A colored servant brought a light, the bell rang, and soon the vessel started down the Potomac, carrying us we knew not where. The bell tolled as we passed the tomb of Washington! Burch, no doubt, with uncovered head, bowed reverently before the sacred ashes of the man who devoted his illustrious life to the liberty of his country.

None of us slept that night but Randall and little Emmy. For the first time Clem Ray was wholly overcome. To him the idea of going South was terrible in the extreme. He was leaving the friends and associations of his youth --everything that was dear and precious to his heart-- and all probability never to return. He and Eliza mingled their tears together, bemoaning their cruel fate. For my own part, difficult as it was, I endeavored to keep up my spirits. I resolved in my mind 100 plans of escape, and fully determined to make the attempt the first desperate chance that offered. I had by this time become satisfied, however that my true policy was to say nothing further on the subject of my having been born a freeman. It would but expose me to maltreatment, and diminish the chances of liberation.

After sunrise in the morning we were called out on deck to breakfast. Burch took our handcuffs off, and we sat down to table. He asked Eliza if she would take a dram. She declined, thanking him politely. During the meal we were all silent- not a word passed between us. A mulatto woman who served at table seemed to take an interest in our behalf- told us to cheer up, and not to be so cast down. Breakfast over, the handcuffs were restored, and Burch ordered us out on the stern deck. We sat down together on some boxes, still saying nothing in Burch's presence. Occasionally a passenger would walk out to where we were, look at us for a while, then silently return.

It was a very pleasant morning. The fields along the river were covered with verdure Far in advance of what I had been accustomed to see at that season of the year. The sun shone out warmly; The birds were singing in the trees. The happy birds-I envied them. I wished for wings like them, that I might cleave the air to where my birdlings waited vainly for their father's coming, in the cooler region of the north.

In the forenoon the steamer reached Aquia Creek. There the passengers took stages-Burch and his five slaves occupying one exclusively. He laughed with the children, and at one stopping place went so far as to purchase them a piece of gingerbread. He told me to hold up my head and look smart. That I might, perhaps, get a good master if I behaved myself. I made him no reply. His face was hateful to me, and I could not bear to look upon it. I sat in the corner, cherishing in my heart the hope, not yet extinct, of someday meeting the tyrant on the soil of my native state.

At Fredericksburg we were transferred from the Stagecoach to a car, and before dark arrived in Richmond, the chief city of Virginia. At this city we were taken from the cars, and driven through the street to a slave pen, between the railroad depot and the river, kept by a Mr. Gooden. This pen is similar to William's in Washington, except it is somewhat larger; And besides, there were two small houses standing at opposite corners within the yard. These houses are usually found within slave yards, being used as rooms for the examination of human chattels by purchasers before concluding a bargain. Unsoundness in a slave, as well as in a horse, detracts materially from his value. If no warranty is given, a close examination is a matter of particular importance to the negro jockey.

We were met at the door of Gooden's yard by that gentleman himself- a short, fat man, with a round, plump face, black hair and whiskers, and a complexion almost as dark as some of his own negroes. He had a hard, stern look, and was perhaps about 50 years of age. Burch and he met with great cordiality. They were evidently old friends. Shaking each other warmly by the hand, Burch remarked he had brought some company, inquired at what time the Brig would leave, and was answered that it would probably leave the next day at such an hour. Goodin then turned to me, took hold of my arm, turned me partly around, looked at me sharply with the air of one who considered himself a good judge of property, and as if estimating in his own mind about how much I was worth.

"Well, boy, where did you come from?"

Forgetting myself, for a moment, I answered, "From New York"

"New York! Hell! What have you been doing up there?" Was his astonished interrogatory.

Observing Burch at this moment looking at me with an angry expression that conveyed a meaning it was not difficult to understand, I immediately said, "Oh, I have only been up that way a piece," in a manner intended to imply that although I might have been as far as New York, yet I wished it distinctly understood that I did not belong to that Free State, nor to any other.

[Burch and Goodin separate]

"You told that man you came from New York," said he.

I replied, "I told him I had been up as far as New York, to be sure, but did not tell him I belong there, nor that I was a free man. I meant no harm at all, master Burch. I would not have said it had I thought."

He looked at me a moment as if he was ready to devour me, then turning round went out. In a few minutes he returned. "If ever I hear you say a word about New York, or about your freedom, I will be the death of you- I will kill you; you may rely on that," he ejaculated fiercely.

I doubt not he understood then better than I did, the danger and the penalty of selling a free man into slavery. He felt the necessity of closing my mouth against the crime he knew he was committing. Of course, my life would not have weighed a feather, in any emergency requiring such a sacrifice. Undoubtedly, he meant precisely what he said.

3—ALBION

Editor–Every school child learns of the Reconstruction period, after the civil war. All the political factions that existed before the civil war, still existed afterwards. The war was over, but the contention continued.

The doubt which Metta had expressed led the Fool, a few days afterwards, to address a grave, wise man, in whose judgment he had always placed much reliance, in order to obtain his views upon the proposed change of domicile. So he wrote to his former college-president, the Rev. Enos Martin, D.D. : —

"MY DEAR OLD FRIEND,-- The fact that I paid so little heed to your monitions when under your charge, is perhaps the reason why I prize your opinion upon any important matter now. I would like to have your views on the question following, promising to weigh them carefully, though I may not act upon them.

" I am considering the idea of removing my household goods to Dixie. So far as my personal characteristics are concerned, you know them better than anyone else probably, except myself, and would not take my own estimate of what you do not know. I can muster a few thousand dollars, —from eight to ten perhaps. I have come out of the war a little the worse for what I have been through; having some trouble in or about one lung; no one seems to know just where, and some other mementos of the affectionate regard of our rebel friends. I find my practice gone, of course, and am a bit afraid of our cold winters. As I desire your views, I will not give mine. Of course, I must burn my bridges if I go. I am too old to face a future containing two upheavals.

" Yours ever,

" COMFORT SERVOSSE."

In a few days there came this answer : —

" MY DEAR COLONEL,.—I am glad to hear you are considering the question stated in your letter. Of course I can not advise you, in the ordinary sense of that word; nor do I suppose you desire that I should. I can only give my general impressions in regard to the future of that part of the country to which you think of removing.

" It is too soon to speculate as to what will be the course of the government in regard to the rebellious sections. A thousand plans are proposed, all of them, as it seems to me, crude, incomplete, and weak. One thing is certain, I think: no one will be punished for rebellion. It is true, Davis and a few others may be invited to go abroad for a few years for the country's good, and perhaps at its expense; but it will end there. There will be no examples made, no reprisals, no confiscation. At the same time, if the results of the war are to be secured, and the nation protected against the recurrence of such a calamity, these States must be rebuilt from the very ground-sill. I am afraid this is not sufficiently realized by the country. I have no idea of any immediate trouble in the South. Such exhaustive revolutions as we have had do not break forth into new life readily. It is the smoldering embers which are to be feared, perhaps a score of years hence. And this can be prevented only by a thorough change in the tone and bent of the people. How much prospect there is of such change being wrought by the spontaneous action of the Southern people, I do not know: I fear, not much.

" It seems to me that the only way to effect it is by the influence of Northern immigration. Of course the old economies of the plantation and the negro-quarters will have to give way. The labor of that Section must be organized, or rather taught to manage itself, to become automatic in its operations. The former master is not prepared to do this; First, because he does not know how; and, secondly, because the freedman has no confidence in his old master's desire to promote his interests. There will be exceptions; but this will be the rule. In this re-organization, I think men who have been acquainted with free (not slave) labor will be able to give valuable aid, and accomplish good re-sults. I look and hope for considerable movements of population be-cause I think it is only by such intermingling of the people of the two sections that they can ever become one, and the danger of future evil be averted. Should the present controversy be concluded, and new States erected in the recently rebellious sections, without a large in-crease of the Northern element in their populations, I am confident that the result will be but temporary, and the future peace of the coun-try insecure.

" As to the social and financial prospects of persons removing there, I suppose it depends very much on the persons themselves, and the particular locality to which they go. I should say you were well fit-ted for such pioneer work; and, if you should conclude to go, I wish you all success and happiness in your new home, and trust that you may find there friends as devoted and sincere as you have hitherto se-cured by an upright and honorable life.

"May God bless you and yours!

" ENOS MARTIN."

By this letter, both the notions of the Fool and the fears of his wife were strengthened. Metta, seeing him grow more and more settled in his determination, did not think it worth while to offer any further opposition; but consoled herself with the reflection that her husband's health was the thing of prime importance, and smothered her fear with a blind, baseless hope, that, because what they purposed doing was a thing born of good motive and kindly feeling, it would be prospered. Some people call that "faith;" and it is no doubt a great, consolation, perhaps the only one, when reason and common sense are squarely opposed to the course one is taking.

4

4-- CORNEIA

The letter below will show the wide difference of travel between then and now. It is addressed to Mrs. Algernon Random (the wife of Mr. Random, of the White Castle), Brunswick County, Virginia, via Richmond and Petersburg.

WOODVILLE, MISSISSIPPI, February 7, 1820.

My Dear Wife:

According to my calculation which I wrote you from Huntsville, Ala., we left there on the evening of the 5th of January, and had a spell of the most inclement weather, through almost the whole way, which had been felt in that region for many years.

The ground was covered with snow when we started, and rain, snow, hail, and ice we had to encounter almost continually, accompanied with severe northwestern winds. It was prophesied by some that we would not reach Natchez until May, and a great many believed we could not possibly get down until March.

The first of February was the day I fixed upon, and accordingly we arrived within eleven miles of Natchez on the 30th of January, where we made a halt, thus making the trip in twenty-five days, with many obstructions to contend with which weather could produce.

And all arrived in good health, without any accident to even one of the horses.

I was, however, very cautious in providing everything necessary for the trip.

The continual exposure to the cold gave me the colic, with which I suffered for several hours very much, but my very good friend Dr.

Egleston was as attentive as it is possible for any human being to be, and finally relieved me.

Since which I have been well, and am at this moment in as good health as I ever experienced, with a great appetite. I have come to this place with all my negroes under the expectation of hiring them all out, should I think proper to do so, to one Col. Gilbert. We had a conversation upon the subject at Natchez, where I met with him, and he was to have met me here several days ago but has not yet arrived, I suppose in consequence of high waters. I expect he will be on this evening, and if we can make a bargain I shall go on immediately to what is here called " The Coast", (Along the river bank from New Orleans, up a hundred miles or so.) to visit that part of the country, return here, and start home about the 20th of this month. Should I make arrangements which may alter that determination I shall advise you of them.

My present intention is to be at Dinwiddie Courthouse, Virginia, on the first Monday in April.

There is not, as to personal security, a safer road in any part of the United States than the Indian Nation through which we passed, nor did we find any difficulty in obtaining supplies when we chose to stay at an Indian house.

We got very good coffee in most places. No beds, but bear skins. I had a large supply of blankets, and my lodgings were comfortable.

A family might live very well by laying in a few articles, such as mattresses, wine, etc.

They would constantly get as much fine venison, fresh or dried, as they could consume, and very often beef, pork, and always chickens. By the route I expect to return I do not expect to be in the Nation more than four or five days, and every night at better stands than are generally found in traveling in many parts of Virginia. Mr. Page and the Doctor are still with me, and seem to be very much pleased with the country. It is a fine country for making money. Cotton is at Orleans from 16 to 18 cents, and as much cotton can be made here to the hand as tobacco in Virginia upon good land. . . . I have met with the kindest reception through the whole country here, every neighbor-hood insisting upon my settling in its vicinity.

Give my love, my dear, to the family.

Your affectionate husband,

ALGERNON RANDOM.

4-- SOLOMON

That night, nearly all who came in [to New Orleans] on the Brig Orleans, were taken ill. They complained of violent pain in the head and back. Little Emily- a thing unusual for her- cried constantly. In the morning a physician was called in, but was unable to determine the nature of our complaint. While examining me, and asking questions touching my symptoms, I gave it as my opinion that it was an attack of smallpox-Mentioning the fact of Robert's death (in Washington) as the reason of my belief. It might be so indeed, he thought, and he would send for the head physician of the hospital. Shortly, the head physician came- a small, light haired man, whom they called doctor Carr. He pronounced it smallpox, whereupon there was much alarm throughout the yard soon after doctor Carr left, Eliza, Amy, Harry and myself were put into a hack and driven to the hospital- a large white marble building standing on the outskirts of the city. Harry and I were placed in a room in one of the upper stories. I became very sick. For three days I was entirely blind. While lying in this state one day, Bob came in, saying to doctor Carr that Freeman had sent him over to inquire how we were getting on. Tell him, said the doctor, that Platt is very bad, but that if he survives until 9:00 o'clock, he may recover.

I expected to die though there was little in the prospect before me worth living for, the near approach of death appalled to me. I thought I could have been resigned to yield up my life in the bosom of my family, but to expire in the midst of strangers, under such circumstances, was a bitter reflection.

There were a great number in the hospital, of both sexes, and of all ages. In the rear of the building coffins were manufactured. When one died, the bell tolled-a signal to the undertaker to come and bear away the body to the Potters field. Many times, each day and night, the tolling bell sent forth its melancholy voice, announcing another death. But my time had not yet come. The crisis having passed, I began to revive, and at the end of two weeks and two days, returned with Harry to the pen, buried upon my face the effects of the melody, which to this day continues to disfigure it. Eliza and Emily were also brought back next day in a hack, and again were we paraded in the sales room, for the inspection and examination of purchasers. I still indulge the hope that the old gentleman in search of a coachman would call again, as he had promised, and purchased me. In that event I felt an abiding confidence that I would soon regain my liberty. Customer after customer entered, but the old gentleman never made his appearance.

At length one day, while we were in the yard, Freeman came out and ordered us to our places, in the great room. A gentleman was waiting for us as we entered, and inasmuch as he will be often mentioned in the progress of this narrative, a description of his personal appearance, and my estimation of his character, at first sight, may not be out of place.

He was a man above the ordinary height, somewhat bent and stooping forward. He was a good looking man, and appeared to have reached about the middle age of life. There was nothing repulsive in his presence; But on the other hand, there was something cheerful and attractive in his face, and in his tone of voice. The finer elements were all kindly mingled in his breast, as anyone could see. He moved about among us, asking many questions, as to what we could do, and what labor we had been accustomed to; if we thought we would like to live with him, and would be good boys if he would buy us, and other interrogatories of like character.

After some further inspection, and conversation touching prices, he finally offered Freeman $1000 for me, 900 for Harry, and 700 for Eliza. Whether the smallpox had depreciated our value, or from what caused Freeman had concluded to fall $500 from the price I was before held at, I cannot say. At any rate, after a little shrewd reflection, he announced his acceptance of the offer.

As soon as Eliza heard it, she was in an agony again. By this time she had become haggard and hollow eyed with sickness and with sorrow. It would be a relief if I could consistently pass over in silence the scene that now ensued. It recalls memories more mournful and affecting than any language can portray. I have seen mothers kissing for the last time the faces of their dead offspring; I have seen them looking down into the grave, as the earth fell with a dull sound upon their coffins, hiding them from their eyes forever; But never have I seen such an exhibition of intense, unmeasured, and unbounded grief, as when Eliza was parted from her child. She broke from her place in the line of women, and rushing down to where Emily was standing, caught her in her arms. The child, sensible of some impending danger, instinctively fastened her hands around her mother's neck, and nestled her little head upon her bosom. Freeman sternly ordered her to be quiet, but she did not heed him. He caught her by the arm and pulled her rudely, but she only clung the closer to the child. Then, with a volley of great oaths, he struck her such a heartless blow, that she staggered backwards, and was like to fall. Oh! How piteously then did she beseech and beg and pray that they might not be separated. Why could they not be purchased together? Why not let her have one of her dear children? "Mercy, mercy, master!" She cried, falling on her knees. "Please, master, buy Emily. I could never work any if she is taken from me: I will die."

Freeman interfered again, but, disregarding him, she still pled most earnestly, telling how Randall had been taken from her- how she never would see him again, and now it was too bad, oh, God! It was too bad, too cruel, to take her away from Emily- her pride- her only darling, that could not live, it was so young, without his mother!

Finally, after much more of supplication, the purchaser of Eliza stepped forward, evidently affected, and said to Freeman he would buy Emily, and asked him what her price was.

"What is her price? Buy her?" Was the responsive interrogatory of Theophilus Freeman. And instantly answering his own inquiry, he added, "I won't sell her period she's not for sale."

The man remarked he was not in need of one so young-that would be of no benefit to him, but since her mother was so fond of her, rather than see them separated, he would pay a reasonable price. But to this humane proposal Freeman was entirely deaf. He would not sell her then on any account whatever. There were heaps and piles of money to be made of her he said, when she was a few years older. There were many enough in New Orleans who would give $5000 for such an extra, handsome, fancy piece as Emily would be, rather than not get her. No, no, he would not sell her then. She was a beauty- a picture- a doll- one of the regular bloods- none of your thick lipped, bullet headed, cotton picking niggers--if she was might he be damned.

When Eliza heard Freeman's determination not to part with Emily, she became absolutely frantic.

"I will not go without her. They shall not take her from me," she fairly shrieked, her shrieks commingling with the loud and angry voice of Freeman, commanding her to be silent.

Meantime Harry and myself had been to the yard and returned with our blankets, and were at the front door ready to leave. Our purchaser stood near us, gazing at Eliza with an expression indicative of regret at having bought her at the expense of so much sorrow. We waited some time, when, finally, Freeman, out of patience, tore Emily from her mother by main force, the two clinging to each other with all their might.

"Don't leave me Mama- don't leave me," screamed the child, as its mother was pushed harshly forward; "Don't leave me- come back, Mama," she still cried, stretching forth her little arms imploringly. But she cried in vain. Out of the door and into the street we were quickly hurried. Still we could hear her calling to her mother, "come back-don't leave me- come back, Mama," until her infant voice grew faint and still more faint, and gradually died away, as distance intervened, and finally was wholly lost.

Eliza never after saw or heard of Emily or Randall. Neither day nor night, however, were they ever absent from her memory. In the cotton field, in the cabin, always and everywhere, she was talking of them- often to them, as if they were actually present. Only when absorbing that illusion, or asleep, did she ever have a moment's comforts afterwards.

4-- *Editor*

After the civil war, federal troops were an occupying force in the South. The program of Reconstruction would begin to take shape. Those in the South who had renounced their US citizenship in aligning with the Confederacy could not regain US citizenship without now taking an oath of allegiance. Confederate money had become worthless, yet that was the only money that many confederates, including plantation owners, had. Many confederate landowners lost their properties. To a large extent, this broke along party lines. The secessionists had been Democrats. The Republican party had formed less than ten years before the civil war, formulated largely from remnants of the Whigs, and of others who were anti-slavery and abolitionist. Lincoln was the first Republican president, and the Northern federals now maintained military rule in the South.

Here is an exchange intended to illustrate the situation. After the civil war was over, but while still commissioned in the army, Servosse was stationed for a period of time in a southern town, as part of the Northern occupation. His job was to oversee the transition back to constitutional civilian government. Temporarily, the military was the law.

4--ALBION

While the matter was in this unsettled state, the Fool received a letter from Colonel Ezekiel Vaughn of Pipersville, a town in which his command had been for some time quartered just before he had quitted the service, to which fact, among other things, he was indebted for the honor of Colonel Vaughn's acquaintance.

Some few days after the collapse of the Confederacy, the gentleman had presented himself at the headquarters of the Fool in Pipersville, and directed the orderly in attendance to announce that, — -

" Colonel Ezekiel Vaughn desired to surrender, and take the oath of allegiance."

Thereupon he was ushered into the presence of our hero, and with considerable pomposity announced the fact again. Somehow, he did not seem to the young soldier to have that air of one accustomed to camps and the usage of armies which was to be expected from a veteran of a four-years' war, who came in at the last moment to give up his sword, after all his comrades had been paroled and had departed. It is true, he had on the regulation gray suit of " the enemy; " and the marks of rank upon the collar might at one time have been intended for the grade he had announced. He wore a light slouch hat, which, though not of any prescribed pattern, had evidently seen much service of some kind. But the surrender brought to light some queer specimens of uniform and equipments, so that Colonel Servosse would not have been surprised at anything that an officer might have worn. There was something, however, in the loud and somewhat effusive greeting, which, even allowing all that it was possible should be credited to laxity of discipline, showed that the man before him was not accustomed to association with military men. So he asked quietly, —

" Of what regiment, sir? "

" Colonel Vaughn, — Colonel Vaughn," said that worthy, depositing himself upon a camp-stool, as if in assertion of his familiarity with military surroundings. " Well, sir," he continued in a loud and somewhat assuming tone, "you've got us, overpowered us at last. It was the Irish and Germans that did it. I had no idea you could get so many of them. They just swarmed on your side. The Yankees never could have whipped us in the world by themselves, never. But it's over. I surrender —give up, — quit. I'm not one of those that want to keep up a fuss always. I've come in to give myself up, and go to work now to try and make bread and meat, sir, — bread and meat. You uns have freed all the niggers, so that we have nobody to work for us. Have to come to it ourselves. Haven't you got a mule you could let me have, Colonel? Hain't got no money; but Zek'le Vaughn's credit's tolerably good yet, I reckon. Lost forty odd niggers, — as likely ones, too, as ever stood 'twixt soil and sunshine, — and now have got to go to plowing at my age. It's hard; but we've got to have bread and meat, — bread and meat, sir. Hard, but can't be helped. Did all I could agin ye ; but here you are. Let me take the oath. - I want to be sworn, and go to plowing before the sun gets too hot."

" What regiment did you say, sir? " repeated the officer.

" Oh, never mind the regiment! " said the other : " that's all over now. Just say Colonel Ezekiel Vaughn: that's enough. Everybody knows Colonel Vaughn, — Zeke Vaughn. I shouldn't wonder if you should find they knew me up at headquarters."

"It is necessary, sir, that I have the name and number of your regiment before you can be paroled," said the officer sharply.

" Ah, yes ! the regiment. Well, Colonel, you are mighty particular, it seems to me. What difference can it make now, I should like to know? " he asked.

" It is necessary to identify you," was the reply.

" Ah, yes ! I see. You are afraid I might break my parole, and give you some trouble. I confess I have not been whipped ; but I am overpowered, -- overpowered, sir, — and I surrender in good faith. I give my honor, sir, — the honor of a Southern gentleman, — as well as my oath, sir! " he said, with a great show of offended dignity.

" That may be, Colonel," responded the officer ; " but our orders require that you shall be fully identified."

"Well, well! that's very proper. Just say Colonel Vaughn of Pipersville : that will identify me. Everybody in the State knows me. No use of my trying to get away. I shall be right here when you want to find me, ready to come up, and be hung, if that is to be the end of it. Oh, I meant it! I was one of the original 'Secesh,'--one of the Immortal 13 that voted for it in this country. I never would have stopped fightin' ye if I'd had my way. You'd never 'a' got here if I'd had my way! But that's all over now. I want my parole, so I can go home, and go to killin' grass!"

Author --Later, as Servosse talks with a local Unioner, that is a southerner with Union sympathies, Servosse asks him about Colonel Vaughn:

"That's what he calls himself; but we mostly calls him 'Zeke Vaughn' or more ginerally just Zeke, or hollerin' Zeke."

"What did he want of exemption-papers?"

"Well,--mostly for the same purpose we all on us did, I reckon!"

"Why, I thought he was an aboriginal Secesh, a regular fire eater!" "So he was at the start, an' in fact all the way through when it was a question of talkin' only; but when it came to fightin' he wan't fire eater enough to want to deprive anyone else of a fair show of the fire. So he got on two sticks (crutches) in the spring of 62, an' hain't been off 'em sence, except to go to bed, 'till last week he went out on his legs into old Polly Richardson's field to keep the Yankees from gobblin' him up."

"He hasn't been in the army, then?"

"Been in the army! Why, bless yer soul! He hasn't seen a Yankee, alive or dead, since the thing begun, till he seed you; an' ef you treat him ez you hev today he's not like tu die tu git a sight of ye agin."

"But isn't he a Colonel?"

"Wal,--not much.

"Then how did he get the title?"

"That would be hard tellin', Mister!"

"Militia Colonel, I suppose."

"I doubt it. Never heard on't ef he was.. I think he jest picked it up ez about 10,000 more in the state hez. Got it by registerin' hisself ez sech hotels, an' givin fellers a drink tu holler fer 'Colonel Ezekiel Vaughn' at perlitical mettin's, an' then answerin' the call."

" Well, what was his exemption-paper, as you call it?"

" Oh! he jest hobbled around on two sticks, pretendin' tu be the worst drawd-up man with rheumatiz you ever seed, till you uns come. You served him right, an' I was glad on't."

In the afternoon several of the leading citizens of the town dropped in, and confirmed indirectly the old Unioner's report in regard to the doughty colonel. They said he was loudmouthed and imprudent; but there was not a bit of harm in him, and he was very much of a gentleman, and of a most respectable family.

So, towards night, he sent an order for the prisoner's release, accompanied by this note addressed to him :

SIR, - Having learned the origin of your title, I have ordered your release, and beg to say that the government of the United States does not consider any parole necessary in your case. You are therefore at liberty to go anywhere you choose.
"

Respectfully,
" COMFORT SERVOSSE,
" Colonel- commanding Post."

The colonel supposed he had seen the last of "Colonel" Vaughn: but in this he reckoned without the "colonel"; for that worthy at once attached himself to his headquarters as a sort of supernumerary orderly and chief volunteer adviser of the young officer. He managed to get a fine team of horses, and made himself indispensable in planning and executing the daily drives into the surrounding country, which the colonel and his officers so much enjoyed as a pleasing contrast to the restraints of a long and arduous campaign. He was a man of great local knowledge, and a sort of good-natured persistency, which induced the impression that he was nothing worse than a well-meaning bore, who was to be endured at all times for the sake of his occasional usefulness and universal cheerfulness.

5

5-- CORNELIA

The income of the master of the White Castle was many thousands a year, owning two plantations; in each about fifteen hundred acres under cultivation and as many more in woodland—very fair dimensions as plantations go—and about five hundred slaves. He and his wife were members of the Episcopal Church, or Church of England, and their children of course were reared in the same faith. The slaves, too, for that matter. Every alternate Sunday afternoon, at their owner's request, they were instructed by the parish minister, for Mr. Random was respected as much for his piety and conscientiousness as for his wealth and intelligence. These services were held at what the negroes called the "meetin' house"—a long, low, frame whitewashed building where they also held their own services on the off Sundays. Then their own preacher would hold forth according to his ideas, no doubt handed down from African traditions, as some of their antics during worship savored of savagery—many shouting themselves into a frenzy, which frequently resulted in a fainting-fit. At this day one colored woman declares she can feel no religion unless she shout. During the week the "meetin' house" was a rendezvous for the darky children of the plantation while the grown people were at work, the babies with a big sister or other child for nurse, and all placed under the care of a general manager, known as " Granny." This smacks of one of the great charities in a large city. Many poor women have no place to leave their offspring where they will be carefully tended when they themselves are at work. The "meetin' house" stood about the center of " the quarters," as the collection of cottages is called where the negroes live.

Each house consisted of two rooms, with shed in front—not painted, but whitewashed—the floors several feet from the ground, and resting on pillars of brick or log. The houses stood in even rows, interspersed with shade trees, and the darkies called the spaces between the rows, streets. They had fireplaces and were far more comfortable than the abode of some well-to-do white people in the old country. At the right side of the quarters was a hospital, where the sick went to he nursed, the family physician receiving so much a year for attentions there, and a good mulatto nurse, Elizabeth Flowers, or " Beth " (for short) , who knew almost as much as the doctor, from association, looked after them. The overseer's house was a stone's throw from the hospital, shut off from view of the family residence by a tremendous sycamore tree. The overseer was general manager, relieving the master of actual work, though acting under orders and reporting the condition of affairs as often as necessary to him, while he (the master) did the mental work and planning, which was considerable, also rode in the fields every morning for an hour or two, except Sundays, to give it a personal supervision. Under the overseer there was usually some trusted slave who saw to menial things, for sometimes the overseer and his family were very respectable, and his children, while children, frequently played with the children of the master, though I never saw a little white girl who did not prefer playing with the pickaninnies when her mother would allow it.

Either the overseer or some reliable foreman rang the large bell in the overseer's yard, which swung from a tall wooden framework, at daylight as the signal for rising. When the field negroes, and all those who were not house servants (these being served from the master's table) were dressed they cooked their own breakfast, which consisted of fried meat, coffee, corn bread, and molasses, of which they are very fond to this day. The midday meal was prepared by persons appointed for the purpose, in the large kitchen at one end of the quarters, the bread baked in an oven outside near by. At this time the big bell rang out the hour, and the meals were distributed all over the fields in tin buckets just from the kitchen. Supper was served in the same manner as breakfast, and the bell sounded the hour for retiring, giving them time for a little gossip among themselves, or occasionally a ball or other amusement. Saturday afternoon the women did the washing and ironing for their families. All being so well looked after, without thought for the morrow, they were very dependent, and not being accustomed to care for themselves their freedom (later on) did not bring what they expected.

At the family residence there was quite a retinue of servants. Phoebie, Patsy, and Ginny were ladies' maids and did the plain sewing by hand for the family, as sewing machines were just being tried and did not work well, or take well—a little of both, perhaps. These maids did as much nodding as sewing as they sat over their work. Patsy, always complaining, was required to do very little and generally accompanied the family, or any member of it, on the various trips that were taken. Her position was a most enjoyable one for anybody, and yet she left her mistress later on, so ignorant was she of what her freedom would bring her, and died soon after in poverty.

5--SOLOMON

On leaving the New Orleans slave pen, Harry and I followed our new master through the streets, while Eliza, crying and turning back, was forced along by Freeman and his minions, until we found ourselves on board the Steamboat Rodolph, then lying at the levee. In the course of half an hour we were moving briskly up the Mississippi, bound for some point on Red River. There were quite a number of slaves on board besides ourselves, just purchased in the New Orleans market. I remember how Mr. Keslow, who was said to be a well known and extensive planter, had in charge a gang of women.

Our master's name was William Ford. He resided then in the "Great Pine Woods," In the parish of Avoyelles, situated on the right Bank of the Red River, in the heart of Louisiana. He is now a Baptist preacher. Throughout the whole parish of Avoyelles, and especially along the shores of Bayou Beuf, where he is more intimately known, he is accounted by his fellow citizens as a worthy minister of God. In many northern minds, perhaps, the idea of a man holding his brother man in servitude, and the traffic in human flesh, may seem altogether incompatible with their conceptions of a moral or religious life. From descriptions of such men as Burch and Freeman, hereinafter mentioned, they are led to despise and execrate the whole class of slaveholders, indiscriminately. But I was some time his slave, and had an opportunity of learning well his character and disposition, and it is but simple justice to him when I say, in my opinion, there never was a more kind, noble, candid, Christian man than William Ford. The influences and associations that had always surrounded him, blinded him to the inherent wrong at the bottom of the system of slavery. He never doubted the moral right of one man holding another in subjugation. Looking through the same medium with his fathers before him, he saw things in the same light. Brought up under other circumstances and other influences, his notions would undoubtedly have been different. Nevertheless, he was a model master, walking uprightly, according to the light of his understanding, and fortunate was the slave who came to his possession. Were all men such as he, slavery would be deprived of more than half its bitterness.

Editor—The slaves complete their trip on the Rodolph. Burch has changed Solomon's name to Platt, in order to make him harder to trace. Solomon, the other slaves, and Ford first take a train, and then at the end of the line, walk to Ford's plantation. Along the way they stop at the summer house of a Mr. Martin, who was a plantation owner who kept a small house in the woods as a retreat.—

We were sent around into the kitchen, and supplied with sweet potatoes, cornbread, and bacon, while master Ford dined with Martin in the house. There were several slaves about the premises. Martin came out and took a look at us, asking for the price of each, if we were green hands, and so forth, and made an inquiries in relation to the slave market generally.

After a long rest we set forth again, following the Texas road, which had the appearance of being very rarely traveled. For five miles we passed through continuous woods without observing a single habitation. At length, just as the sun was sinking in the West, we entered another opening, containing some 12 or 15 acres.

In this opening stood a house much larger than Mr. Martins. It was two stories high, with a piazza in front. In the rear of it was also a log kitchen, poultry house, and several negro cabins. Near the house was a Peach orchard, and gardens of orange and pomegranate trees. The space was entirely surrounded by woods, and covered with a carpet of rich, rank verdure. It was a quiet, lonely, pleasant place- literally a green spot in the wilderness. It was the residence of my master, William Ford.

As we approached, a yellow girl-her name was Rose- was standing on the piazza. Going to the door, she called her mistress, who presently came running out to meet her Lord. She kissed him, and laughingly demanded if he had bought "those niggers." Ford said he had, he told us to go around to Sally's cabin and rest ourselves. Turning the corner of the house, we discovered Sally washing her two baby children near her, rolling on the grass. They jumped up and toddled towards us, looked at us a moment like a brace of rabbits, then ran back to the mother as if afraid of us.

Sally conducted us into the cabin, told us to lay down our bundles and be seated, before she was sure that we were tired. Just then John, the cook, a boy some 16 years of age, and blacker than any crow, came running in, looked steadily in our faces, then turning round, without saying as much as "how d'ye do," ran back to the kitchen, laughing loudly, as if our coming was a great joke indeed.

Much wearied with our walk, as it was dark, Harry and I wrapped our blankets around us, and laid down upon the cabin floor. My thoughts, as usual, wander back to my wife and children. The consciousness of my real situation; the hopelessness of any effort to escape through the wild forest of Avoyelles, pressed heavily upon me, yet my heart was at home in Saratoga.

I was awakened early in the morning by the voice of Master Ford, calling Rose. She hastened into the house to dress the children, Sally to the field to milk the cows, while John was busy in the kitchen preparing breakfast. In the meantime Harry and I were strolling about the yard, looking at our new quarters. Just after breakfast a colored man, driving three yoke of oxen, attached to a wagon load of lumber, drove into the opening. He was a slave of Fords, named Walton, the husband of rose. By the way, rose was a native of Washington, and had been brought from thence five years before. She had never seen Eliza, but she had heard of Berry, and they knew the same streets, and the same people, either personally, or by reputation. They became fast friends immediately, and talked a great deal together of old times, and of friends they had left behind.

Ford was at that time a wealthy man. Besides his seat in the Pine Woods, he owned a large lumbering establishment on Indian Creek, four miles distant, and also, in his wife's right, an extensive plantation and many slaves on Bayou Boeuf.

Walton had come with his load of lumber from the mills of Indian Creek. Ford directed us to return with him, saying he would follow us as soon as possible. Before leaving, mistress Ford called me into the store room, and handed me, as it is there termed, a tin bucket of molasses for Harry and myself.

Eliza was still ringing her hands and deploring the loss of her children. Ford tried as much as possible to console her- told her she need not work very hard; that she might remain with rose, and assist the Madam in the house affairs.

Riding with Walton in the wagon, Harry and I became quite well acquainted with him long before reaching Indian Creek. He was a "born thrall" of four words, and spoke kindly and affectionately of him, as a child would speak of his own father. In answer to his inquiries from whence I came, I told him from Washington. Of that city, he had heard much from his wife, Rose, and all the way plied me with many extravagant and absurd questions.

On reaching the mills at Indian Creek, we found two more of Ford's slaves, Sam and Anthony. Sam, also, was a Washingtonian, having been brought out in the same gang with Rose. He had worked on a farm near Georgetown. Anthony was a blacksmith, from Kentucky, who had been in his present master's service about 10 years. Sam knew Burch, and when informed that he was the trader who had sent me on from Washington, it was remarkable how well we agreed upon the subject of his superlative rascality. He had forwarded Sam, also.

On Ford's arrival at the mill, we were employed in piling lumber, and a chopping logs, which occupation we continued during the remainder of the summer.

We usually spent our sabbaths at the opening, on which days our master would gather all his slaves about him, and read and expound the scriptures. He sought to inculcate in our minds feelings of kindness towards each other, of dependence on God-setting forth the rewards promised unto those who lead in upright and prayerful life. Seated in the doorway of his house, surrounded by his man servants and his maid servants, who looked earnestly into the good man's face, he spoke of the loving kindness of the creator, and of the life that is to come. Often did the voice of prayer ascend from his lips to heaven, the only sound that broke the solitude of the place.

In the course of the summer Sam became deeply convicted, his mind dwelling intentionally on the subject of religion. His mistress gave him a Bible, which he carried with him to his work. Whatever leisure time was allowed him, he spent in perusing it, though it was only with great difficulty that he could master any part of it. I often read to him, a favor which he well repaid me by many expressions of gratitude. Sam's piety was frequently observed by white men who came to the mill, and the remark it most generally provoked was, that a man like Ford, who allowed his slaves to have Bibles, was "not fit to own a nigger".

He, however, lost nothing by his kindness. It is a fact I have more than once observed, that those who treated their slaves most leniently, were rewarded by the greatest amount of Labor. I know it from my own experience. It was a source of pleasure to surprise master Ford with a greater day's work than was required, while, under subsequent masters, there was no prompter to extra effort but the overseer's lash.

It was the desire of Ford's approving voice that suggested to me in idea the result to his profit. The lumber we were manufacturing was contracted to be delivered at Lamourie. It had hitherto been transported by land, and was an important item of expense. Indian Creek, upon which the mills were situated, was a narrow but deep stream emptying into Bayou Bouef. In some places it was not more than 12 feet wide, and much obstructed with trunks of trees. Bayou Bouef was connected with Bayou Lamourie. I ascertained the distance from the mills to the point on the latter bayou, where our lumber was to be delivered, was but a few miles less by land than by water. Provided the Creek could be made navigable for rafts, it occurred to me that the expense of transportation would be materially diminished.

Adam Taydem, a little white man, who had been a soldier in Florida, and had strolled into that distant region, was foreman and Superintendent of the mills. He scouted the idea; but Ford, when I laid it before him, received it favorably, and permitted me to try the experiment.

Having removed the obstructions, I made-up a narrow raft, consisting of 12 cribs. At this business I think I was quite skillful, not having forgotten my experience years before on the Champlain canal. I labored hard, being extremely anxious to succeed, both from a desire to please my master, and to show Adam Taydem that my scheme was not such a visionary one as he Damn it incessantly pronounced it. One hand could manage three cribs. I took charge of the forward three, and commenced polling down the Creek. In due time we entered the first bio, and finally reached our destination in a shorter period of time than I had anticipated.

The arrival of the raft at Lamourie created a sensation, while Mr. Ford loaded me with commendations. On all sides I heard Ford's Platt pronounced the "smartest nigger in the Pine Woods"-In fact I was the Fulton of Indian Creek. I was not insensible to the praise bestowed upon me, and enjoyed, and especially, my triumph over Taydem, whose half-malicious ridicule had stung my pride. From this time the entire control of bringing the lumber to Lamourie was placed in my hands until the contract was fulfilled.

5—ALBION

Author – Servosse has purchased Warrington, a plantation much in need of repair after the civil war.

The following is a letter that Metta has written to her sister.

"My dear friend Julia,--I do not know how I can better employ a few hours of Thanksgiving Day than in writing you the promised letter of our new home and our journey here. While you are shivering with cold, perhaps looking out upon ice and snow, I am sitting upon a little veranda, over which clamors rose vine still wreathed with buzz and blossoms. There has been a slight frost; and those on the outside are withered, but those within are yet as fresh as if it were but a June. The sun shines warmly in, and everything without is touched with that delicious haziness which characterizes the few peculiar autumn days of the north that we call Indian summer. There is the same soft, dreamy languor, and the same sense of infinite distance around us.

"Everybody and everything is new to us; that is, to Lily and me. Comfort's four years of soldier life made him very familiar with similar scenes; And I, I doubt not, a large part of our enjoyment comes from having him to explain all these wonders to us.

"It did seem terribly lonely and desolate when we first arrived. You know comfort had come before, and completed the purchase, and made some preparations for our reception; That is, he had engaged somebody to make the preparations, and then returned for us. We had a fearful journey,--rough seas and rickety boats, a rough country, and railroads which seem to lack all that we have considered the essentials of such structures the rails were worn and broken, the crosstie sunken and decayed; while every now and then we would see where some raiding party had heated the rails, and twisted them around trees, and their places had been supplied with old rusty pieces taken from some less important track. Comfort said he believed they would run the train on 'the right of way' alone pretty soon. All through the country were the marks of war,--forts and earthworks and stockades. Army wagons, ambulances, and mules are scattered everywhere, and seem to be about all the means of transportation that are left. The poor confederacy must have been on its last legs when it gave up.

"The last 12 hours of the trip it rained,--rained as you never saw it, as I think it never can rain except in this climate. To say that it poured, would give you but a faint idea of it. It did not beat or blow: there was not a particle of storm, or anything like excitement or exertion about it. It only fell--steadily, quietly, and uninterruptedly. It seemed as if the dull, heavy atmosphere were shut in by an impenetrable canopy of clouds, and laden with an exhaustive list amount of water, just sufficiently condensed to fall. There was no patter, but one ceaseless sound of falling water, almost like the sheet of a cascade in its weight and monotony, on the roof of the old leaky car. In the midst of this rain, at midnight, we reached the station nearest to Warrington. It is, in fact, a Pretty Little town of 2000 or so inhabitants; but it was as dark as the catacombs, and as quiet, save for the rain falling, falling everywhere, without intermission. The conductor said there was a good hotel, if we could get to it; but there was no vehicle of any kind, and no light at the station except the conductors Lantern, and a tallow candle flickering in the little station house.

"Comfort got our baggage off, and stored in the station house, after a deal of trouble; And with bags and boxes on our arms, hand muffled up to the chin to keep out the rain (which seemed to come through an umbrella as if it scorned such an attempt to divert it from

its course), we started for the hotel under the pilotage of the conductor with his Lantern. Such a walk! Has comfort helped me out of the
car, he said, 'it's fearfully muddy.' He need not have said it. Already I
was sinking, sinking, into the soft, tenacious mass. Rubbers were of
no avail, nor yet at the high shoes I had put on in order to be expressly prepared for whatever might await me. I began to fear quick-
sand; And, if you had seen my clothing the next morning, you would
not have wondered. Luckily it was dark, and no one can ever more
than guess what a draft a procession we made that night."

"And then the hotel; but I spare you that! Lily cried herself to sleep,
and I came very near it.

"The next morning the earth was as bright and smiling as if a del-
uge had not passed over it and a few hours before. Comfort was all
impatience to get out to Warrington, and we were as anxious to leave
that horrible hotel. So he got an ambulance, and we started. He said
he had no doubt our goods were already there, as they had been sent
on three weeks before, and he had arranged with a party to take them
out to the plantation. At least, he said, we could not be worse off than
we were at that wretched hotel, in which I fully agreed with him; but
he did not know what was in store for us!

Warrington is only 6 miles from the station; but we were two
mortal hours in getting there with our trunks and the boxes we had
brought with us. Think of riding through mud almost as red as blood,
as sticky as pitch, and deeper than plummet ever told, for two hours,
after an almost sleepless night and a weary journey of seven days, and
you may faintly guess with what feelings I came to Warrenton. As we
drove up the avenue under the grand old oaks, just ripening into a
state and sober brown, interspersed with hickories which were one
blaze of gold from the lowest to the topmost branch, and saw the Gray
squirrels (which the former owner would not allow to be killed, and
no one had had time to kill since) playing about, and the great brick
house standing in silent grandeur amid this mimic forest, I could have
kissed the trees, the squirrels, the weather beaten portrait, the muddy

earth itself, with joy. It was home,-- rest. Comfort saw the tears in my eyes, the first which I had shed in it all, and said tenderly,--

"There, there! It's almost over!' As if I had been a tired baby.

Lily was in rapture over the beauties of the old place, yes indeed she had good right to be; but I was tired. I wanted rest. We drove to the house, and found it empty,--desolate. The doors were open; the water had run across the hall; everything was so barron that I could only sit down and cry. After some trouble comfort found the man who was to have made the repairs And brought the goods. He said the goods had not come, and he 'llowed there wa'n't no use fixing things 'till they come.

Comfort sent the ambulance which brought us out to go get some provisions, a few cooking utensils, and some other absolute necessities. A colored woman was found, who came in, and, with the many willing hands which she soon summoned to her aid, made the house (or one room of it) quite cozy. However things have been coming by piece meal ever since, and we are now quite comfortable.

Comfort has bought me a riding horse,--a beautiful blooded Bay mare; and he has his old War Horse, Lollard, which he had left in this vicinity with an old man named Jehu Brown,,--who, by the way, is a character,--having an impression that we might come here. So we ride a great deal. The roads are so rough that it is difficult to get about in any other way; and it is just delightful riding through the wood-paths, and the curious crooked country roads by day or night.

The people here seem very kind and attentive. A good many gentlemen have called to see Comfort. They are all 'Colonels' or 'Squires', and very agreeable, pleasant men. A few ladies have called on me,--always with their husbands though; and I think they are inclined to be less gracious in their manner, and not so cordial in their welcome, as the gentlemen. I notice that none of them have been very pressing in their invitations for us to return their courtesy. Comfort says it is not at all to be wondered at, but that we ought rather to be surprised and pleased that they come at all; and I do not know but he is right.

Two or three countrymen came to see comfort a few days after our arrival. They were all misters, not 'colonels' and 'squires'. They said they were union men; and it was wonderfully interesting to hear them tell, in their quaint provincialism, what happened to them during the war.

We rode out to see one of them afterwards, and found him a thrifty farmer, with four or five hundred acres of good land, living in a log home, with a strange mixture of plainness and plenty around him. Somehow I think I shall like this class of people better than the other,-- though they are rough and plain,-- they seem so very good hearted and honest.

We are going to have the teachers from the colored school at Verdenton here to dinner today to keep Thanksgiving. There are some full half dozen of them,-- all northern girls. I have not met them; But Comfort says they are very pleasant ladies. Of course, they have no society except a few northern people; and he is going to bring them out to give them a treat as well as ourselves, I suppose.

Yours ever, with love to all,

Metta

6

6—— **CORNELIA**

The field negroes' clothes were cut out and made for them by negro women whose business it was. Sometimes the mistress did the cutting, which kept her busy, with all her other household cares, and the hospitalities which she was expected to maintain. Any of them now living, I am sure, feel it a relief to have the care of them off their hands. When the clothes were finished the darkies put them on and went to the mistress to express their satisfaction or pass their criticism on the comfort and fit. The house servants made their own garments and dressed well, often remodeling the cast-off clothing of the family, which was probably only slightly soiled, and because of their fine feathers thought themselves above the field hands, and were inclined to put on airs, forming the aristocracy of the black population. Sunday developed their resources in finery. Meely would mince along looking, or trying to look, very coquettish under a pink silk parasol given her by young miss," and beaming with smiles, hanging on the arm of Yaller Jack, " who was sporting a silk hat of " ole marsteh's " and twirling a cane cut from the osage hedge that skirted the plantation—in fine, aping the gentleman. They were field hands, but called into the house or yard in emergencies. Saturday night those who wished could dance in the " meetin' house " to the tune of a fiddle, but if those danced who belonged to " de chuch " Minerva would expose them and administer stern justice by " turnin'em out."

6—SOLOMON

Indian Creek, in its whole length, flows through a magnificent forest. There dwells on its shore a tribe of Indians, a remnant of the

Chickasaws or Chicopee 's, if I remember rightly. They live in simple huts, 10 or 12 feet square, constructed of pine poles and covered with bark. They subsist principally on the flesh of the deer, the racoon, and opossum, all of which are plenty in these woods. Sometimes they exchange venison for a little corn and whiskey with the planters on the bayous. Their usual dress is buckskin breeches and calico hunting shirts off fantastic colors, button from belt to chin. They wear brass rings on their wrists, and in their ears and noses. The dress of the squaws is very similar. They are fond of dogs and horses-owning many of the latter, of a small, tough breed and are skillful riders. Their bridles, girths and saddles were made of raw skins of animals; their stirrups of a certain kind of wood. Mounted astride their ponies, men and women, I have seen them dash out into the woods at the utmost of their speed, following narrow winding paths, and dodging trees, in a manner that eclipsed the most miraculous feats of civilized equestrianism. Circling away in various directions, the forest echoing and reechoing with their hoops, they would presently return at the same dashing, headlong speed with which they started. Their village was on Indian Creek, known as Indian Castle, but their range extended to the Sabine River. Occasionally a tribe from Texas would come over on a visit and then there was indeed a carnival in the "Great Pine Woods". Chief of the tribe was Cascalla; second in rank, John Baltese, his son-in-law; with both of whom, as with many others of the tribe, I became acquainted during my frequent voyages down the Creek with rafts. Same in myself would often visit them when the day's task was done. They were obedient to the chief; the word of Cascolla was their law. They were a rude but harmless people, and enjoyed their wild mode of life. They had little fancy for the open country, the cleared lands on the shores of the bayous, but prefer to hide themselves within the shadows of the forest. They worshipped the great spirit, loved whiskey, and were happy.

On one occasion I was present at a dance, when a roving heard from Texas had encamped in their village. The entire carcass of a deer was roasting before a large fire, which threw its light a long distance along the trees under which they were assembled. When they had formed a ring, men and squaws alternatively, a sort of Indian fiddle set up on indescribable tune. It was a continuous, melancholy kind of wavy sound, with the slightest possible variation. At the first note, if indeed there were more than one note in the whole tune, they circled around, trotting after each other, and giving utterance to a gutteral, sing-song noise, equally as nondescript as the music of the fiddle. At the end of the Third Circuit, they would stop suddenly, whoop as if their lungs would crack, then break from the ring, forming in couples, man and squaw each jumping backwards as far as possible from the other, then forwards-Which graceful feat Having been twice or thrice accomplished, they would form in a ring, and go trotting around again. The best dancer appeared to be considered the one who could whoop the loudest, jump the farthest, and utter the most excruciating noise. At intervals, one or more would leave the dancing circle, and going to the fire, cut from the roasting carcass a slice of venison.

In a hole, shaped like a mortar, cut in the trunk of a fallen tree, they pounded corn with a wooden pestle, and of the meal made cake. Alternately they danced and ate. Thus were the visitors from Texas entertained by the dusky sons and daughters of the Chicopee, and such is a description, as I saw it, of an Indian ball in the Pine Woods of Avoyelles.

In the autumn, I left the mills, and was employed at the opening. One day the mistress was urging Ford to procure a loom, in order that Sally might commence weaving cloth for the winter garments of the slaves. He could not imagine where one was to be found, when I suggested that the easiest way to get one would be to make it, informing him at the same time, that always a sort of "Jack of all trades", and would attempt it, with his permission. It was granted very readily, and I was allowed to go to a neighboring planter's to inspect one before commencing the undertaking. At length it was finished and pronounced by Sally to be perfect. She could easily weave her task of 14 yards, milk the cows, and have leisure time besides each day. It works so well, I was continued in the employment of making looms, which were taken down to the plantation on the Bayou.

At this time one John M Tibeats a Carpenter, came to the opening to do some work on master's house. I was directed to quit the looms and assist him. For two weeks I was in his company, planing and matching boards for a ceiling, a plastered room being a rare thing in the parish of Avoyelles.

John M Tibeats was the opposite of Ford in all respects. He was a small, crabbed, quick-tempered, spiteful man. He had no fixed residence that I ever heard of, but passed from one plantation to another, wherever he could find employment. He was without standing in the community, not esteemed by white men, nor even respected by slaves. He was ignorant, with all, and of a revengeful disposition. He left the parish long before I did, and I know not whether he is at present alive or dead. Certain it is, it was a most unlucky day for me that brought us together. During my residence with master Ford I had seen only the bright side of slavery. His was no heavy hand crushing us to the earth. He pointed upwards, and with benign and cheering words addressed us as his fellow mortals, accountable, like himself, to the Maker of us all. I think of him with affection, and had my family been with me, could have borne his gentle servitude, without murmuring, all my days. But clouds were gathering in the horizon-forerunners of a pitiless storm that was soon to break over me. I was doomed to endure such bitter trials as the poor slave only knows, and to lead no more the comparatively happy life which I had led in the "Great Pine Woods".

6-- ALBION

Editor –Another letter from Metta:

"My dear Julia,--my last letter to you was written while I was waiting for the young ladies, who are teaching at Verdenton, to come and share our Thanksgiving dinner. That was a momentous day for us, and at that dinner our most important affair. We were a little short of some things necessary for such an occasion; but we pierced and fitted, and, with the help of the willing hands of many colored girls (you must remember that all colored women are 'girls') , we made out to spread a very respectable table. Comfort had gone into town early with my little bridal-wise mare Jaca, in leading for one of the young ladies to ride; and the ambulance followed for the others. Just as my letter was finished, they all came up the avenue to the house; and a merrier crowd I am sure I never saw in my life. Six sweeter girls could not be found. They are employed by the Missionary Associations two teach in the colored schools that have sprung up all over the South like magic, and are real missionaries in the very best sense of the word. They are from six different States, and never saw each other until they met here at the school in Verdenton, and are all cultivated, refined ladies of the best class of our Northern people, who have come here simply to do good. It was really charming to see them, so fresh and, girlish, just from loving homes and tender friends, coming away down here on a noble errand, where they are despised and insulted for the very good they perform. Only the few Northern people who are here will have any thing to . do with them. They are as much missionaries, and have as much to undergo, as if they were in Turkey deed more, if our old friend who is teaching in Beirut tells the whole truth in regard to her difficulties. We had a delightful day ; and towards night both of us returned with them, and sending back the ambulance, and keeping only our saddle-horses, staid at the Mission House, as their abode is called, until after nine o'clock; and then Comfort and I rode home in the moonlight. I don't think I was ever happier in my life, or felt that I had been the cause of more happiness to others, than on that day ; and, when we knelt for our evening prayer, I did thank God with all my heart that he had directed our steps hitherward, for I believe we have a blessed work to do, and that our lives here will not be in vain.

" A few days afterward I went to call on some of the ladies who had visited me. It was so far that Comfort went with me, and I persuaded him to let me go on horseback ; for it is so unpleasant to ride in an ambulance, which is the only alternative. This would not be quite en regle at home, I know; but here it is a very general thing, and it is a mode of traveling too delightful ever to be abandoned. We called at three houses, and were received at all of them with a very marked restraint of manner, and with positive rudeness in one case. I felt as if I could cry from disappointment and chagrin. We wanted to be friendly, and avoided every subject of conversation which could give pain ; and it seemed too bad to be met with such coolness. Comfort tried to console me as we rode home but I could see that he felt it as well as I. " A day or two after this, Squire Hyman, who is one of our nearest neighbors, though he lives a mile away, came over to see us. He is a queer old gossip, who is so anxious to be on good terms with everybody that he has hard times to keep anybody on his side. During the war, it seems, he played fast and loose; and it is amusing enough to hear Colonel Vaughn and his Confederate friends caution us against him as a man who professed to be all right,' but was all the time encouraging deserters and harboring bushwhackers ; and then to hear Jehu Brown, and other known and reliable Unionists, say, He won't du tu tie ter. He was always claimin' tu be a powerful good Union man, an' at the same time givin' information agin any o' the boys that was hidin' out.'

"I knew that he had something ' very particular,' as he says, to tell the moment he came into the room ; but it was a long time before he could get to it. I think Comfort suspected what it was, and purposely led him away from the point he was striving to reach. At length he bounced it squarely,' as the country-people hereabout say, with the statement, —

"' I hear they've got a powerful big school for the— the niggers as we call them, — in Verdenton.'

" Oh, yes ! ' I answered in all innocence. ' We had the young ladies who are teaching there out here to our Thanksgiving dinner, and liked them very much.'

" Indeed! I don't know any thing about them, good or bad. Of course I hear a good deal said ; but that's neither here nor there. Some folks make a heap of fuss about every thing; but I'm one of them that lets other folks alone if they don't trouble me. That's right, ain't it, Colonel ? He, he ! '

" I don't see why there should be any thing said against these young ladies,' said I.

" Well,' he replied, you know how we Southern people are. We have our own notions.' And he winked, and chuckled to himself ; and I said rather sharply, —

"' I don't see what your notions have to do with these young ladies, who are certainly doing God's work in teaching these poor colored people, old and young.'

" 'Oh, certainly! it would look so ; but—'

"'But what ?" said Comfort so markedly that the old man jumped in his seat.

"Nothing — that is — nothing of account only—you know, Colonel, we can't help thinking that any one that comes from the North down here, and associates with niggers — can't — well -- can't be of much account at home.'

" And you call teaching colored people associating with them? " asked Comfort.

" Well, of course, in a manner,' answered the squire hesitatingly.

" And you doubtless think it disreputable to associate with such teachers?'

" Well, Colonel, I'm glad you mentioned it. I didn't want to broach it myself, being a delicate subject, you know ; but it is so counted — by — the best society, you know.'

" So you came to warn us that if we continue to associate with these teachers we must forego the pleasures of good society here-abouts? '

" Well, I had heard remarks, you know. I name no names; but I thought it would be no more than neighborly, being as you were strangers as I may say. and not accustomed to our ways, to let you know, so that you might be careful in the future.'

" Thank you. We are certainly under many obligations to you for letting us know whom we are to be permitted to associate with, and whom not.'

" Oh, not at all ! not at all 1 I'm sure it's no more than I would do for any neighbor,' said the squire with an air of gratified vanity.

" Certainly not, Squire,' said Comfort sarcastically, — and I knew from the flashing of his eyes that some one would get a shot, — certainly not ; and it is my confidence in your neighborly inclination which makes me presume to ask a favor at your hands.'

" Any thing in the world that I can do, sir. I'm sure I shall be proud to serve you,' said the squire with marked enthusiasm.

"' Then, Squire, I would be glad if you would say to these good people who have undertaken to regulate our associations, that I bought this property, paid for it cash down, and am quite capable of regulating my own affairs without their aid."

" What do you mean, sir? ' said the squire, starting from his seat, white with rage. ' Do you mean to insult me ?'

" I mean,' said Comfort quietly, to say that the ladies who are teaching in the colored school at Verdenton are ladies of character and culture, fit associates for my wife, and fully the equals of any lady in the State. I desire to say further, that, regarding them as such, if it comes to a choice between ostracizing them simply because of the good work in which they are engaged, and losing the approval of the first families of Verdenton and vicinity, I shall certainly choose the latter.'

" Well — of course,' said the squire, somewhat staggered by this view of the matter, of course you have a right to your own way. I meant no harm, not the least in the world. Good-evening, sir ! Good-evening, Madam!' And her was gone to-do the errand at Comfort's bidding.

" Colonel Vaughn came the next day upon the same errand. I did not hear the conversation he had with Comfort ; but he talked very loud, and I suppose was answered much as the squire had been. I heard Comfort say to him, just as he was leaving, —

" I fought four years, sir, for the privilege of living under the flag of the United States with all the rights of a citizen in any part of the Union, and I do not intend to permit anybody to dictate my conduct towards anybody else.' .

" If your family associate with nigger teachers, you can not expect respectable people to recognize them as associates.'

" We do not ask anybody to associate with us, sir. We are not suppliants for recognition. If people desire our friendship, we are frank and outspoken, pretending to nothing more than we are, and accepting others as we find them. If they do not wish to associate with us, we do not complain, and are not likely to mourn.'

" The colonel, as he calls himself, went away in high dudgeon;

7

7-- CORNELIA

There were quite a number of what were called " free ne-groes," enough to form a little circle of society among themselves, for though respected they did not mix socially with the whites. They had the same advantages as the upper circle, owned slaves, had large plan-tations—some of them getting educated in France—and were so wealthy that when the daughter of the most prominent was married her father presented her with an eighteen hundred dollar bedstead and a thousand dollar bracelet.

The German professor who made the rounds in the neighborhood as music teacher gave her lessons on the piano, and remarked that she had talent, but her hands were too small to stretch an octave.

She had a nice wedding, but the beautiful bed¬stead with its four elaborately carved posts and damask canopy was too high for her room in the low French house, and the attic floor above had to be raised to admit it. Such is the story as the professor gave it.

These colored planters were acquainted with French literature and spoke the French language among themselves ; were known by their first names, without any prefix. Of course when they lost their slaves, like their white neighbors, they lost their all. Some of them were quick to seize the opportunity politics offered. Being educated, they became prominent leaders among their race, and drew the salaries of honorable positions, with large perquisites never before or since known to belong to the office. The more scrupulous fell back upon their various accomplishments to make a bare living for themselves.

7-- SOLOMON

I was now compelled to labor very hard period from earliest dawn until late at night, I was not allowed to be a moment idol. Notwithstanding which, Tibeats was never satisfied. He was continually cursing and complaining. He never spoke to me a kind word. I was his faithful slave, and earned him large wages every day, and yet I went to my cabin nightly, loaded with abuse and stinging epithets.

We had completed the cornmeal, the kitchen, and so forth, and were at work upon the weaving-house, when I was guilty of an act, in that state punishable with death. It was my first fight with Tibeats. The weaving-house we were erecting stood in the orchard a few rods from the residence of Chapin, or the "great house" as it was called. One night, having worked until it was too dark to see, I was ordered by Tibeats to rise very early in the morning, procure a keg of nails from Chapin, and commence putting on the clapboards. I retired to the cabin extremely tired, and having cooked a supper of bacon and corn cake, and conversed a while with Eliza, who occupied the same cabin, as also did Lawson and his wife Mary, and a slave named Bristol, laid down upon the ground floor, little dreaming of the sufferings that awaited me on the morrow. Before daylight I was on the piazza of the great house awaiting the appearance of overseer Chapin. To have aroused him from his slumbers and stated my errand, would have been an unpardonable boldness. At length he came out. Taking off my hat I, informed him Master Tibeats had directed me to call upon him for a keg of nails. Going into the storeroom, he rolled it out, at the same time saying, if Tibeats preferred a different size, he would endeavor to furnish them, but that I might use those until further directed. Then mounting his horse, which stood saddled and bridled at the door, he rode away into the field, whither the slaves had preceded him, while I took the keg on my shoulder, and proceeding to the weaving house, broke in the head, and commenced nailing on the clapboards.

As the day began to open, Tibeats came out of the house to where I was, hard at work. He seemed to be that morning even more morose and disagreeable than usual. He was my master, entitled by law to my flesh and blood, and to exercise over me such tyrannical control as his mean nature prompted; but there was no law that could prevent my looking upon him with intense contempt. I despised both his disposition and his intellect. I had just come round to the keg for further supply of nails, as he reached the weaving house.

"I thought I told you to commence putting on weather boards this morning," he remarked.

"Yes, master, and I am about it," I replied

"Where?" He demanded.

"On the other side," was my answer.

He walked round to the other side, examined my work for a while, muttering to himself in a fault finding tone.

"Didn't I tell you last night to get a keg of nails of Chapin?" He broke forth again.

"Yes, master, and so I did; and overseer said he would get another size for you, if you wanted them, when you came back from the field."

Walked to the keg, looked a moment at the contents, then kicked it violently. Coming towards me in a great passion he exclaimed, "G-d d—m you! I thought you *knowed* something."

I made answer: "I tried to do as you told me, master. I didn't mean anything wrong. Overseer said—" But he interrupted me with such a flood of curses that I was unable to finish the sentence. At length he ran towards the house, and going to the piazza, took down one of the overseers whips. The whip had a short wooden stock, braided over with leather, and was loaded at the butt. The lash was 3 feet long, or thereabouts, and made of rawhide strands.

At first I was somewhat frightened, and my impulse was to run. There was no one about except Rachel, the cook, and Chapin's wife, and neither of them were to be seen. The rest were in the field. I knew he intended to whip me, and it was the first time anyone had attempted it since my arrival at Avoyelle. I felt, moreover, that I had been faithful- that I was guilty of no wrong whatever, and deserved commendation rather than punishment. My fear changed to anger and before he reached me I had made up my mind fully not to be whipped, let the result be life or death.

Winding the lash around his hand, and taking hold of the small end of the stock, he walked up to me, and with a malignant look, ordered me to strip.

"Master Tibeats", said I, looking him boldly in the face, "I will *not*." I was about to say something further in justification, but with concentrated vengeance, he sprang upon me, seizing me by the throat with one hand, raising the whip with the other, in the active striking. Before the blow descended, however, I had caught him by the collar of the coat, and drawn him closely to me. Reaching down, I seized him by the ankle, and pushing him back with the other hand, he fell over on the ground. Putting one arm around his leg, and holding it to my breast, so that his head and shoulders only touched the ground, I placed my foot upon his neck. He was completely in my power. My blood was up. It seemed to course through my veins like fire. In the frenzy of my madness I snatched the whip from his hand. He struggled with all his power; swore that I should not live to see another day; and that he would tear up my heart. But his struggles and his threats were alike in vain. I cannot tell how many times I struck him. Blow after blow fell fast and heavy upon his wriggling form. At length he screamed- cried murder- and at last the blasphemous tyrant called on God for mercy. But he who had never shown mercy did not receive it. The stiff stock of the whip warped around his cringing body until my right arm ached.

Until this time I had been too busy to look about me. Desisting for a moment, I saw Mrs. Chapin looking from the window, and Rachel standing in the kitchen door. Their attitudes expressed the utmost excitement and alarm. His screams had been heard in the field. Chapin was coming as fast as he could ride. I struck him a blow or two more, then pushed him from me with such a well-directed kick that he went rolling over on the ground.

Rising to his feet, and brushing the dirt from his hair, he stood looking at me, pale with rage. We gazed at each other in silence. Not a word was uttered until Chapin galloped up to us.

"What is the matter?" He cried out.

"Master Tibeats wants to whip me for using the nails you gave me," I replied.

"What is the matter with the nails" he inquired, turning to Tibeats?

Tibeats answered to the effect that they were too large, paying little heed, however, to Chapin's question, but still keeping his snakish eyes fastened maliciously on me.

"I am overseer here," Chapin began. "I told Platt to take them and use them, and if they were not of the proper size I would get others on returning from the field. It is not his fault. Besides, I shall furnish such nails as I please. I hope you will understand that, Mr. Tibeats."

Tibeats made no reply, but, grinded his teeth and shaking his fist, swore he would have satisfaction, and that it was not half over yet. Thereupon he walked away, followed by the overseer, and entered the house, the latter are talking to him all the while in a suppressed tone, and with earnest gestures.

I remained where I was, doubting whether it was better to fly or abide the result, whatever it might be. Presently Tibeats came out of the house and, saddling his horse, the only property he possessed besides myself, departed on the road to Chenyville.

When he was gone, Chapin came out, visibly excited, telling me not to stir, not to attempt to leave the plantation on any account whatever. He then went to the kitchen, and calling Rachel out, conversed with her sometime. Coming back, he again charged me with great earnestness not to run, saying my master was a rascal; That he had left on no good errand, and that there might be trouble before night. But at all events, he insisted upon it, I must not stir.

As I stood there, feelings of unalterable agony overwhelmed me. I was conscious that I had subjected myself to unimaginable punishment. The reaction that followed my extreme ebullition of anger produced the most painful sensations of regret. An unfriended, helpless slave-what could I do, what could I say, to justify, in the remotest manner, the heinous act I had committed, of resenting a white man's contumely and abuse. I tried to pray-I tried to beseech my Heavenly Father to sustain me in my sore extremity, but emotion choked my utterance, and I could only bow my head upon my hands and weep. For at least an hour I remained in this situation, finding relief only in tears, when, looking up, I beheld Tibeatsts accompanied by two horsemen, coming down the Bayou. They rode into the yard jumped from their horses, and approached me with large whips, one of them also carrying a coil of rope.

"Cross your hands," commanded Tibeats, With the addition of such a shuddering expression of blasphemy as is not decorous to repeat.

"You need not bind me, Master Tibeatsts, I am ready to go with you anywhere, said I".

One of his companions then stepped forward, swearing if I made the least resistance he would break my head- he would tear me limb from limb- he would cut my black throat-and giving wide scope to other similar expressions. Perceiving any importunity altogether vain, I crossed my hands, submitting humbly to whatever disposition they might please to make of me. They're upon the Tibeats tied my wrists, drawing the rope around them with his utmost strength. Then he bound my ankles in the same manner. In the meantime the other two had slipped a cord within my elbows, running it across my back, and trying it firmly. It was utterly impossible to move hand or foot. With a remaining piece of rope Tibeats made an awkward noose, and placed it about my neck.

"Now, then," inquired one of Tibeat 's companions," where shall we hang the nigger?"

One proposed of such a limb, extending from the body of a Peach tree, near the spot where we were standing. His comrade objected to it, alleging it would break, and proposed another. Finally they fixed upon the latter.

During this conversation, and all the time they were binding me, I uttered not a word. Overseer Chapin, during the progress of the scene, was walking hastily back and forth on the Piazza. Rachel was crying by the kitchen door, and Mrs. Chapin was still looking from the window. Hope died within my heart. Surely my time had come. I should never behold the light of another day--never behold of the faces of my children--the sweet anticipation I had cherished with such fondness. I should that hour struggle through the fearful agonies of death! None would mourn for me-- none revenge me. Soon my form would be moldering in that distant soil, or, perhaps, be cast to the slimy reptiles that filled the stagnant waters of the bayou! Tears flowed down my cheeks, but they only afforded a subject of insulting comment from my executioners.

At length, as they were dragging me toward the tree, Chapin, who had momentarily disappeared from the Piazza, came out of the house and walked towards us. He had a pistol in each hand, and as near as I can now recall to mind, spoke in a firm, determined manner, as follows:

"Gentlemen, I have a few words to say. You had to better listen to them. Whoever moves that slave another foot from where he stands is a dead man. In the first place, he does not deserve this treatment. It is a shame to murder him in this manner. I never knew a more faithful boy than as Platt. You, Tibeats, are in the fault yourself. You are pretty much of a scoundrel, and I know it, and you richly deserve the flogging you have received. In the next place, I have been an overseer on this plantation seven years, and, in the absence of William Ford, am master here. My duty is to protect his interest, and that duty I shall perform. You are not responsible--you are a worthless fellow. Ford holds a mortgage on Platt of $400. If you hang him he loses his debt.

Until that is cancelled you have no right to take his life. You know you have no right to take it anyway. There is a law for the slave as well as for the white man. You are no better than a murderer.

"As for you," Addressing Cook and Ramsay: a couple of overseers from neighboring plantations "as for you-- be gone! If you have any regard for your own safety, I say, be gone."

Cook and Ramsey, without a further word, mounted their horses and rode away. Tibeats, in a few minutes, evidentially in fear, and overawed by the decided tone of Chapin, sneaked off like a coward, as he was, and mounting his horse, followed his companions.

I remained standing where I was, still bound, with a rope around my neck. As soon as they were gone, Chapin called Rachel, ordering her to run to the field, and tell Lawson to hurry to the house without delay, and bring the brown mule with him, an animal much praised for its unusual fleetness. Presently the boy appeared.

"Lawson," said Chapin, "you must go to the Pine Woods. Tell your master Ford to come here at once--that he must not delay a single moment. Tell him they are trying to murder Platt. Now hurry, boy. Be at the pine woods by noon if you kill the mule.

Chapin stepped into the house and wrote a pass. When he returned, Lawson was at the door, mounted on his mule. Receiving the pass, he applied the whip right smartly to the beast, dashed out of the yard, and turning up the bayou on a hard gallop, in less time than it has taken me to describe the scene, was out of sight.

7—ALBION

Editor--Metta continues her letter. Local newspapers were a prime form of communication in a time before telephones, radio, or television. Thus, local newspapers contained more than mere fact-based stories, in order to keep people informed of social concerns.

...and the next week the paper published at Verdenton had a dirty little squib in regard to the matter, which I send you. It read as follows : —

'Our readers will regret to learn that the Canadian Yankee .Servosse, who has bought the Warrington Place, is one of those fanatical abolitionists whose infamous doctrines were the real cause of all the suffering and bloodshed of the last four years. Our citizens had extended many favors to him, and our ladies had shown very marked courtesy to his family. Instead of appreciating these things, he has chosen to slander our first ladies by comparing them with the nigger schoolmarms who have come down here to teach social equality by example.

We understand that Servosse had all these free-love nigger-missionaries of the female persuasion out at Warrington to celebrate the new Yankee holiday, which has been added to the governmental calendar since the first year of Lincoln's reign, called Thanksgiving Day. The day itself is a relic of New-England Puritanical hypocrisy, and, we understand, was fitly observed at Warrington, where they ate and drank, and sung " John Brown," " We're coming, Father Abraham," and similar melodies. It is said that one of the "N. T.'s " became so full of the spirit of the occasion, that she kissed one of the colored boys who waited at the table. Colonel Servosse cannot expect his family to be recognized by respectable people if he chooses such associates for them.'

" Did you ever see any thing so mean ? Of course we don't care any thing about it : only one likes to live peaceably with one's neighbors if possible. Comfort was very much exasperated when he first saw this, and went into town in a very angry mood. I don't know what he did; but the next week there was a very abject apology in the paper. It made a great excitement though, and even many of the colored people advised us not to have the teachers here any more. (' N. T.,' you know, is Southern euphemism for Nigger Teacher.) Of course we paid no attention to it, and will have them here just as often as we can, both to show that we are not moved by such things, and because they enjoy coming so much.

" Some time ago Comfort concluded to establish a sabbath school for colored people, as there are a great many in this neighborhood, and no school of any kind for them nearer than Verdenton. So he consulted with some of their leading men, and they fixed up an arbor and some seats in a grove not far from the house ; and you ought to see what congregations gather there Sunday afternoons. Two or three white men came in at first, as if to see what would be done. Comfort asked them to take classes, and help us teach these poor people. One old man with long, white hair, strange, dark eyes, and a mild, soft voice, came forward, and said that it was a good work, and he thanked God that he had put it into the mind of this new neighbor to do it ; and he for one would do all in his power to assist him.

" The others stood off, and did not seem to know what to do about the matter. The old man's name is George D. Garnet. He is of Huguenot descent, and belongs to a large family in the South, whose name has been corrupted from its original orthography. He is very proud of his descent, and was attracted to us by our name being also French. He is a deacon of the Baptist church in Mayfield, about twenty miles from here. He says he has been trying to get his church to take hold of a colored sabbath school from the very day of the surrender; but they will not hear him. He has often staid to tea with us, and we find him very entertaining indeed. He is very eccentric, as is evident from what he says, and the stories the colored people tell of him. He says he was a slaveholder who thought slavery wrong, — a Virginia abolitionist,' as he says. The colored people say that he used to buy slaves who were anxious to be free, and let them work out- their A —dom. He was not a rich man, only just a good common as they say ; but in this way he bought and freed many slaves.

The colored people flock around us as if they thought de Yankee, kunnel ' could do every thing, and hire them all. I think I could have a hundred housemaids if I would take all that come to me, and Lilian has nurses enough offered to take charge of all the children in your town.

Comfort has decided to sell all of Warrington but 100 acres. The rest lies along the creek, and is very well fitted to cut up into little farms of 10 and 20 acres for colored men, giving them upland to live on, with a little timber, and a nice piece of good bottom to cultivate. He is going to put little log houses on them, and sell them to colored people on 6 or 10 years time. It will make quite a little town.

We hope to do some good, and trust that the foolish prejudice of the people will wear away. It is strange how treacherous they are, though. An old country woman, who came along with some things to sell the other day, said she had heard that the Colonel had come down here to try and put the niggers over the white folks, and want to know if it was true! She had a snuff stick in her mouth, and neither she nor her two grown daughters could read or write! It is wonderful how many there are here who are so ignorant; and those who are not ignorant are full of a strange prejudice against all who are notoft their own particular set, and think and believe just as they do.

There are some reports of difficulties experienced by northern men in some parts of the South; but we hope they are exaggerated.

8

8-- **CORNELIA**

Richard Random, the owner of the White Castle and the broad lands I have described, was commanding in height, with the air of a patrician nobly defined, and of a Saxon type. To describe his true nature I can best use the words of a friend and close observer.

" Among characters, one who my experience of life and people has taught me to esteem at his full value is the master of the White Castle ; imbued with pride, yet unpretentious, thrifty, purely honest, and shedding all the sunshine of his nature into his own home and upon his own family. The very sim¬plicity of his character invested it with greatness. Others laid claims to fame, but when j ustice places the wreath of nobility of character she will lay it upon the grave of this one." As for the mistress, Dean Stanley once met her and remarked that for elegance of bearing and grace of manner she equaled any English duchess he had ever met. In repose she was stately, otherwise vivacious, with a remarkable degree of energy and courage, which the war developed to a heroic point and belied the prevalent Northern idea of the indolent Southern women. She was descended from the French marquis mentioned elsewhere. Without any apparent effort she had full command of the servants, impressing them so forcibly with the idea of her vigilance they said she seemed to have eyes in the back of her head. Yet she was so kind in all their troubles they looked on her as a friend. I have seen her sitting up at night, after the war, making clothes for negro babies whose mothers were shiftless.

There were nine children in the Random family, Robert and Algernon, eighteen and sixteen respectively, Patricia and Penelope, eight and five, children of Mr. and Mrs. Richard Random ; two of Mr. Random's orphaned nieces (his sister Cordelia's children), Adelaide and Isabel, sixteen and fourteen, and Richard, Eugenia, and Bertha, ten, five, and three, motherless children of Mr. Random's brother William and Mrs. Random's sister Bertha. Mr. William Random was consul in foreign parts. Julia and Richard came between Algernon and Patricia, but they died in their infancy. One can easily conceive how happy and prosperous was this family when the storm broke upon the South, changing all the old ways, making them but a vague reminiscence.

8-- SOLOMON

Early the next morning, Tibeats left the plantation. In the course of the forenoon, while sauntering about the gin house, a tall, good looking man came to see me, and inquired if I was Tibeat's boy, that youthful appellation from being applied indiscriminately to slaves even though they may have passed the number of three score years and 10. I took off my hat, and answered that I was.

"How would you like to work for me?" He inquired.

"Oh, I would like to, very much," said I, inspired with a sudden hope of getting away from Tibeats.

"You worked under Myers at Peter Tanners, didn't you?"

I replied I had, adding some complimentary remarks that Myers had made concerning me.

"Well, boy," said he, "I have hired you of your master to work for me in the" Big Cane Break, 38 miles from here, down on Red River."

This man was Mr. Eldret, who lived below Ford's, on the same side of the bayou. I accompanied him to his plantation, and in the morning started with his slave Sam, and a wagon load of provisions, drawn by 4 mules, for the Big Cane, Eldret and Myers having preceded us on horseback. This Sam was a native of Charleston, where he had a mother, brother and sisters. He "allowed"--a common word among both black and white--that Tibeats was a mean man, And hope, as I most earnestly did also, that his master would buy me.

We proceeded down the South Shore of the bayou, crossing it at Carey's plantation; from thence to Huff Power, passing which, we came upon the Bayou Rouge road, which runs down towards Red River. After passing through Bayou Rouge swamp, and just at sunset, turning from the highway, we struck off into the "Big Cane Break." We followed an unbeaten track, scarcely wide enough to admit the wagon. The cane, such as are used for fishing rods, were as thick as they could stand. A person could not be seen through them the distance of a rod. The paths of wild beast run through them in various directions--the bear and the American tiger are abounding in these breaks, and wherever there is a basin of stagnant water, it is full of alligators.

We kept on our lonely course through the Big Cane several miles, when we entered a clearing, known as Sutton's Field." Many years before, a man by the name of Sutton had penetrated the wilderness of Cain to this solitary place. Tradition has it, that he fled thither, a fugitive, not from service, but from justice. Here he lived alone--recluse and hermit of the swamp--with his own hands planting the seed and gathering in the harvest. One day a band of Indians stole upon his solitude, and after a bloody battle, overpowered and massacred him. For miles the country round, in the slaves quarters, and on the piazzas of great houses, where white children listen to superstitious tales, the story goes, that that spot, in the heart of the Big Cane is a haunted place. For more than 1/4 of a century, human voices had rarely, if ever, disturbed the silence of the clearing. Rank and noxious weeds had overspread the once cultivated field--serpents sunned themselves on the doorway of the crumbling cabin. It was indeed a jury picture of desolation.

Passing "Suttons Field," We followed a new cut road 2 miles farther, which brought us to which termination. We had now reached the wild lands of Mr. Eldret, where he contemplating clearing up an extensive plantation. We went back to work next morning with our cane knives, and cleared a sufficient space to allow the erection of two cabins--one for Myers and Eldret, the other for Sam, myself, and the slaves that were to join us. We were now in the midst of trees of enormous growth, whose wide spreading branches almost shut out the light of the sun, while the space between the trunks was an impervious mass of cane, with here and there an occasional Palmetto.

The Bay and the Sycamore, the oak and the Cypress, reach a growth unparalleled, in those fertile lowlands bordering the Red River. From every tree, moreover, hang long, large masses of moss, presenting to the eye unaccustomed to them, a striking and singular appearance. This moss, in large quantities, is sent north, and they're used for manufacturing purposes.

We cut down oaks, split them into rails, and with these erected temporary cabins. We covered the roofs with broad Palmetto leaf, an excellent substitute for shingles, as long as they last.

The greatest annoyance I met with here were small flies, gnats and mosquitoes. They swarmed the air. They penetrated the porches of the ear, the nose, the eyes, the mouth. They sucked themselves beneath the skin. It was impossible to brush or beat them off. It seemed, indeed, as if they would devour us-- carry us away piece meal, in their small tormenting mouths.

How lonely your spot, or one more disagreeable, then the center of the "Big Cane Break," It would be difficult to conceive; yet to me it was a paradise, in comparison with any other place in the company of master Tibeats. I labored hard, and oft-times was weary and fatigued, yet I could lie down at night in peace, and in the morning rise without fear.

In the course of a fortnight, four black girls came down from Eldridge plantation-- Charlotte, Fannie, Cresia and Nelly. They were all large and stout. Axes were put into their hands, and they were sent out with Sam and myself to cut trees. They were excellent choppers, their largest oak or Sycamore standing but a brief season before they're heavy and well directed blows. At piling logs, they were equal to any man. There are lumber woman as well as lumber men in the forests of the South. In fact, in the region of the Bayou Bouef they perform their share of all the labor required on the plantation. They plow, drag, drive team, clear wild lands, work on the highway, and so forth. Some planters, owning large cotton and sugar plantations, have none other than the labor of slave women. Such an one is Jim Burns, who lives on the North Shore of the bayou, opposite the plantation of John Fogaman.

On our arrival in the break, Eldret promised me, if I worked well, I might go up to visit my friends at Fords in four weeks. On Saturday night of the 5th week, I reminded him of his promise, when he told me I had done so well, that I might go. I had set my heart upon it, and Eldret's announcement thrilled me with pleasure. I was to return in time to commence the labours of the day on Tuesday morning.

While indulging the pleasant anticipation of so soon meeting my old friends again, suddenly the hateful form of Tibeatts appeared among us. He inquired how Myers and Platt Yeah got along together, and was told, very well, and that Platt was going up to Ford's plantation in the morning on a visit.

"Poh, poh!" Sneered Tibeats; "it isn't worthwhile--the nigger will get unsteady. He can't go."

But Eldret insisted I had worked faithfully-- they had given me his promise, and that, under the circumstances, I ought not to be disappointed. They then, it being about dark, entered one cabin and I the other. I could not give up the idea of going; It was a sore disappointment. Before morning I resolved, if Eldret made no objection, to leave at all hazards. At daylight I was at his door, with my blanket rolled up into a bundle, and hanging on a stick over my shoulder, waiting for a pass. Tibbetts came out presently in one of his disagreeable moods, washed his face, and going to a stump nearby, sat down upon it, apparently busily thinking with himself. After standing there a long time, impelled by a sudden impulse of impatience, I started off.

"Are you going without a pass?" He cried out to me.

"Yes, master, I thought I would," I answered.

"How do you think you'll get there?" demanded he.

"Don't know," was all the reply I made to him

"You'd to be taken and sent to jail, where you ought to be, before you got halfway there," he added, passing into the cabin as she said it. He came out soon with a pass in his hand, and calling me a "dammed nigger that deserved 100 lashes," threw it on the ground. I picked it up, and hurried away right speedily.

A slave caught off his masters plantation without a pass, may be seized and whipped by any white man whom he meets. The one I now received was dated, and read as follows:

"Platt has permission to go to Ford's Plantation, on Bayou Boeuf, and return by Tuesday morning.

John M Tibeats"

This is the usual form. On the way, a great many demanded it, read it, and passed on. Those having the air and appearance of gentlemen, whose dress indicated the possession of wealth, frequently took no notice of me whatever; Shabby fellow, an unmistakable loafer, never failed to hail me, and to scrutinize and examine me in the most thorough manner. Catching runaways is sometimes a money making business. If, after advertising, no owner appears, they may be sold to the highest bidder; and certain fees are allowed the Finder for his services, had all events, even if reclaimed. "A mean white," Therefore,-- a name applied to the species loafer—considers it a godsend to meet an unknown negro without a pass.

8—ALBION

He became an object of remark at public assemblies; the newspaper at Verdenton had every now and then sliding allusions to him; and the idea was industriously circulated that he was somehow connected—identified—with "Yankee power," and had been sent to the South for some sinister motive. He was not one of them. He represented another civilization, another development, of which thou were naturally suspicious, and especially so on account of the peculiar restrictions which slavery had put around them, kind which had acted as an embargo on immigration

The intercourse between his family and those who constitute what was termed "good society" gradually dwindled, without actual rudeness or tangible neglect, until the few country-people who "neighbored with them," as it is termed there, comprised their only society, if we except the teachers of the colored school and the few Northern families in the town.

Now and then this feeling of hereditary aversion for the Yankee manifested itself unpleasantly; but it was usually only an undemonstrative, latent feeling, which was felt rather than seen in those with whom he associated in business or otherwise, until the first year had passed away, and the crops had been gathered.

Little attention had been paid to the manner in which he had chosen to build houses and sell lands to the colored people, — it being perhaps regarded as merely a visionary idea of the Yankee abolitionist. When, however, the crops were harvested, and some of these men became owners of horses and houses in their own right, it seemed all at once to awaken general attention. One night a gang of disguised ruffians burst upon the little settlement of colored men, beat and cruelly outraged some, took the horses of two, and cut and mangled those belonging to others.

When the Fool arose the next morning, he found the following, attached to his door-knob, wrapped in a piece of black cloth on which was traced in white paint a death's-head and crossbones above the figure of a coffin : —

" COLONEL COMFORT SERVOSSE. Sir, — You hev got to leeve this country, and the quicker you do if the better ; fer you ain't safe here, nor enny other miserable Yankee ! You come here to put niggers over white folks, sayin ez how they should vote and set on juries and swear away white folks rites as much as they damn please. You are backin up this notion by a sellin of em land and hosses and mules, till they are gittin so big in ther boots they cant rest. You've bin

warned that sech things wont be born ; but you jes go on ez if ther
want nobody else on arth. Now, we've jes made up our minds not to
stan it enny longer. We've been and larned yer damn niggers better
manners than to be a ridin hossback when white, folks is walkin. The
Regulators hez met, and decided thet no nigger shant be allowed to
own no hoss nor run no crop on his own account hereafter. And no
nigger-worshipin Yankee spy thet encourages them in their insolence
shel live in the county. Now, sir, we gives you three days to git away.
Ef your here when that time's over, the buzzards will hev a bait that's
been right scarce since the war was over. You may think we's foolin.
Other people hez made that mistake to ther sorrer. Ef you don't want
to size a coffin jest yit you better git a ticket that will take you towards
the North Star jes ez far ez the roads been cut out.

" By order of

THE CAPTAIN OF THE REGULATORS."

The Fool at once published this letter in " The Verdenton Gazette,"
with a short, sturdy answer, saying that he was minding his own business, and expected other people to mind theirs. He paid for it as an
advertisement. — the only terms on which the editor would admit it
to his columns. This proceeding, which in the North or in any other
state of society would have awakened the liveliest indignation towards those who thus attempted to drive him away from his home. as
well as a strong sympathy for him, had no such effect upon this community. Many openly approved the course of the mob; others faintly
condemned; and no one took any steps to prevent the consummation
of the outrage threatened. No one seemed to think that the Fool was
entitled to any support or sympathy. That he should sell land to colored men, and assist them to purchase stock, was considered by nearly
the entire community as an offence deserving the worst punishment;
and that he should go farther, and publicly favor their enfranchisement, was such a gross outrage upon the feelings and prejudices of the
whites, that many seemed much surprised that any warning at all had
been given by the "Regulators".

The one most interested, however, was not idle. He procured arms and ammunition, and prepared for the defense of his life and property, and the protection of his tenants and those to whom he had sold. A stockade was built for the horses in a favorable position, a guard provided, and signals agreed on in case of an attack. The commandant of the troops at a neighboring station sent a small detachment, which remained for a few days, and was then withdrawn. They had not been required by the owner of Warrington; but the rumor went out that he had called for troops to protect him, and the feeling grew day by day more hostile towards him.

9

9-- CORNELIA

There were rumors and rumors of war and the superstitious thought it was predicted in the sky, for one summer night the whole canopy of the heavens was obscured by mottled clouds which were tinged with color as red as blood. Such a phenomenon had not been seen before by those who saw it then, nor has it been seen since. Then there were comets which the negroes were quite sure would end the world, and so it seemed for them—for subsequent events opened up a new world they had not hitherto dreamed of. Speaking figuratively, the ominous clouds burst and deluged the beautiful land with blood.

When Mr. Random heard the enemy were near he took many of his slaves to a secluded spot in Texas, to keep them together until the war should be over. He also took some furniture and handsome glass and china, to help establish another home in case of necessity for his family during this time. On his arrival he purchased a place in the interior, upon which he and his slaves lived comfortably. He then told them that he would let the issues of the war decide their final disposal, that he in the meantime would be a good master to them and hoped they would give him no trouble, that some of them were separated from their families just as he was from his, but that all who wished it would be reunited in due time.

Mrs. Random remained on the home plantation with the children and continued to carry it on with

the remaining slaves, hoping their presence would save it from destruction. When she saw the great armed ships moving stealthily along the river, viewing their recent acquisitions, she put a dagger in her belt and went on the front gallery to watch the unknown foe. Some of the officers were later entertained and cordial relations established, to be followed up after the war. Mrs. Random was not without trepidation herself at this time, however, and the children were quite sure all their heads would be cut off, though they went out to look on too. For the present nothing was molested, but when some Confederates passed in front on the public road—then the bombs burst around the house, sending a bullet crashing through a window with such force it went through the wall on the other side of the room, and putting several in the posts on the veranda, also scattering them over the floor, where they fell rolling around the occupants' feet. When the shelling became too fierce the basement was sought as the safest place--there was company in the house, as there usually is in a Southern home. When they heard the cannon booming and saw the ground torn up around them, the children, who were out in the meadow with old Minerva, began to cry, so she tucked them under a bridge near by, thinking it a safe place, and got under herself, cautiously peeping out to watch the situation from time to time.

The shelling followed the troops, who were passing, and later the bombs fell at some other place, when Minerva with her frightened brood saw her way safe to the house and arrived (breathless with excitement) much to the relief of Mrs. Random.

9--SOLOMON

There are no ends along the highways in the portion of the state where I sojourned. I was wholly destitute of money, neither did I carry any provisions, on my journey from the Big Cane to Bayou Boeuf; Nevertheless, with his pass in his hand, a slave need never suffer from hunger or from thirst. Only necessary to present it to the master or overseer of a plantation, and state his wants, when he will be sent round to the kitchen and provided with food or shelter, as the case may require. The traveler stops at any house and calls for a meal with as much freedom as if it was a public tavern. General custom of the country. Whatever their faults may be, it is certain the inhabitants along Red River, and around the bayous in the interior of Louisiana are not wanting in hospitality.

I arrived at Ford's plantation towards the close of the afternoon, passing in the evening in Eliza's cabin, with Lawson, Rachel, and others of my acquaintance. When we left Washington Eliza's form was round and plump. She stood erect, and in her silks and jewels, presented a picture of graceful strength and elegance. Now she was but a thin shadow of her former self. Her face had become gastly haggard, and the once straight and active form was bowed down, as if bearing the weight of 100 years. Crouching on her cabin floor, and clad in the coarse garments of a slave, old Elisha Berry would not have recognized the mother of his child. I never saw her afterwards. Having become useless in the cotton field, she was bartered for a trifle, to some man residing in the vicinity of Peter Compton's. Brief head nod remorsefully at her heart, until her strength was gone; and for that, her last master, it is said, lashed and abused her most unmercifully. But he could not whip back the departed vigor of her youth, nor straighten up the bended body to its full height, such as it was when her children were around her, and the light of freedom was shining on her path.

I learned the particulars relative to her departure from this world, from some of Compton's slaves, who had come over Red River to the Bayou, to assist young Madam Tanner during the "busy season." She became at length, they said, utterly helpless, for several weeks lying on the ground floor in a dilapidated cabin, dependent upon the mercy of her fellow thralls for an occasional drop of water, and a morsel of food. Her Master did not" knock her on the head," as is sometimes done to put a suffering animal out of misery, but left her unprovided for, and unprotected, to linger through a life of pain and wretchedness to its natural close. When the hands returned from the field one night they found her dead! During the day, the Angel of the Lord, remove with invisibly over all the earth, gathering in his harvest of departing souls, had silently entered the cabin of the dying woman, and taken her from thence. She was *free* at last!

Next day, rolling up my blanket, I started on my return to the Big Cane. After traveling 5 miles, had a place called Huff Power, the ever present Tibeats met me in the road. He inquired why I was going back so soon, and when informed I was anxious to return by the time I was directed, he said I need go no farther than the next plantation, as he had that day sold me to Edwin Epps. We walked down into the yard, where we met the latter gentleman, who examined me, and asked me the usual questions propounded by purchasers. Having been duly delivered over, I was ordered to the quarters, and at the same time directed to make a hoe and axe handle for myself.

I was now no longer the property of Tibeats--His dog, his brute, trading his wrath and cruelty day and tonight; and whoever or whatever my new master might prove to be, I could not, certainly, regret the change. So it was good news when the sale was announced, and with a sigh of relief I sat down for the first time in my new abode. Tibeats soon after disappeared from that section of the country. Once afterwards, and only once, I caught a glimpse of him. It was many miles from Bayou Boeuf. He was seated in the doorway of a low groggery. I was passing, in a drove of slaves, through St. Mary's parish.

Edwin Epps, of whom much will be said during the remainder of this history, is a large, portly, heavy bodied man with light hair, high cheekbones, and a Roman nose of extraordinary dimensions. He has blue eyes, a fair complexion, and is, as I should say, full six feet high. He has the sharp, inquisitive expression of a jockey. His manners are repulsive and coarse, and his language gives speedy and unequivocal evidence that he has never enjoyed the advantages of an education. He has the faculty of saying most provoking things, in that respect even excelling old Peter Tanner. At the time I came into his possession, Edwin Epps was fond of the bottle, his "sprees" sometimes extending over the space of two whole weeks. Loud early, however, he had reformed his habits, and when I left him, was as strict a specimen of temperance as could be found on Bayou Boeuf. When "in his cups," Master Epps was a roistering, blustering, noisy fellow, whose chief delight was in dancing with his "niggers," or lashing them about the yard with his long whip, just for the pleasure of hearing them screech and scream, as the great Welt were planted on their backs. When sober, he was silent, reserved and cunning, not beating us indiscriminately, as in his drunken moments, but sending the end of his rawhide to some tender spot of a lagging slave, with the sly dexterity peculiar to himself. He had been a driver and overseer in his younger years, but at this time was in possession of a plantation on Bayou Huff Power, 2 1/2 miles from Holmesville, 18 from Marksville, and 12 from Cheneyville. It belonged to Joseph B Roberts, his wife's uncle, and was leased by Epps. His principal business was Raising cotton, and inasmuch as some may read this book who have never seen a cotton field, a description of the manner of its culture may not be out of place.

The ground is prepared by throwing up beds or ridges, with a plow—back-furrowing, it is called. Oxen and mules, the latter almost exclusively, are used in plowing. The woman as frequently as the men performed this labor, feeding, currying, and taking care of their teams, and in all respects doing the field and stable work, precisely as to the ploughboys of the North.

The beds, or ridges, are six feet wide, that is, from water furrow to water furrow. A plow drawn by one mule is then run along the top of the Ridge or center of the bed, making the drill, into which a girl usually drops the seed, which she carries in a bag hug around her neck. Behind her comes a mule and harrow, covering up the seed, so that two mules, three slaves, a plow and harrow, are employed in planting a row of cotton. This is done in the months of March and April. Corn is planted in February. When there are no cold rains, the cotton usually makes its appearance in a week. In the course of eight or ten days afterwards the first hollowing has commenced. This is performed in part, also, by the aid of the plow and mule. The plow passes as near as possible to the cotton on both sides, throwing the furrow from it. Slaves follow with their hose, cutting up the grass and cotton, leaving hills 2 feet and a half apart. This is called scraping cotton. In two weeks more commences the second hoeing. This time the furrow is thrown towards the cotton. Only one stock, the largest, is now left standing in each hill. In another fortnight it is hoed the third time, throwing the furrow towards the cotton in the same manner as before, and killing all the grass between the rows. About the 1st of July, when it is a foot high or there abouts, it is so the fourth and last time period now the whole space between the rows is plowed, leaving a deep water furrow in the center. During all these hoeings the overseer or driver follows the slaves on horseback with a whip, such as has been described. The fastest power takes the lead row. He is usually about a rod in advance of his companions. If one of them passes him, he is whipped. If one falls behind or is a moment idle, he is whipped. In fact, the lash is flying from morning until night, the whole day long. The hoeing season thus continues from April until July, a field having no sooner been finished once, than it is commenced again.

In the latter part of August begins the cotton picking season. At this time each slave is presented with a sack. A strap is fastened to it, which goes over the neck, holding the mouth of the sack breast high, while the bottom reaches nearly to the ground. Each one is also presented with a large basket that will hold about two barrels. This is to put the cotton in when the sack is filled. The baskets are carried to the field and placed at the beginning of the rows.

When a new hand, one unaccustomed to the business, is sent for the first time into the field, he is whipped up smartly, and made for that day to pick as fast as he can possibly. At night it is weighed, so that his capability in cotton picking is known. He must bring in the same weight each night following. If he falls short, it is considered evidence that he has been laggard, and a greater or lesser number of lashes is the penalty.

In ordinary day's work is 200 pounds. A slave who was accustomed to picking, is punished, if he or she brings in less quantity than that. There is great difference among them as regards this kind of Labor. Some of them seemed to have a natural neck, or quickness, which enables them to pick with great celebrity, and with both hands, while others, with whatever practice or industry, are utterly unable to come up with the ordinary standard. Such hands are taken from the cotton field and employed in other business. Patsy, of whom I shall have more to say, was known as the most remarkable cotton picker on Bayou Boeuf. She picked with both hands and with such surprising rapidity, that 500 pounds a day was not unusual for her.

Each one is tasked, therefore, according to his picking abilities, none, however, to come short of 200 weight. I, being unskillful always in that business, would have satisfied my master by bringing in the latter quantity, while on the other hand, Patsy would surely have been beaten if she failed to produce twice as much.

The cotton grows from five to seven feet high, each stalk having a great many branches, shooting out in all directions, and lapping each other above the water furrow.

There are few sites more pleasant to the eye, than a wide cotton field when it is in bloom. It presents an appearance of purity, like an Immaculate expansive light, new fallen snow.

Sometimes the slave picks down one side of a row, and back upon the other, but more usually, there is one on either side, gathering all that has blossomed, Leaving the unopened bolls for a succeeding picking. When the sack is filled, it is emptied into the basket and trodden down. It is necessary to be extremely careful the first time going through the field, in order not to break the branches off the stalks. The cotton will not bloom upon a broken branch. Epps never failed to inflict this furious chastisement on the unlucky servant who, either carelessly or unavoidably, was guilty in the least degree in this respect.

The hands are required to be in the cotton field as soon as it is light in the morning, and, with the exception of 10 or 15 minutes, which is given them at noon to swallow their allowances of cold bacon, they are not permitted to be a moment to idle until it is too dark to see, and when the moon is full, they oftentimes labor till the middle of the night. They do not dare to stop even at dinner time, nor return to the quarters, however late it may be, until the order to halt is given by the driver.

The day's work over in the field, the baskets are "toted," or in other words, carried to the gin house, where the cotton is weighed. No matter how fatigued and where he may be-- no matter how much he longs for sleep and rest-- a slave never approaches the gin house with his basket of cotton but with fear. If it falls short in weight--if he has not performed the full task appointed him, he knows that he must suffer. And if he has exceeded it by 10 or 20 pounds, in all probability his master will measure the next day's task accordingly so, whether he has too little or too much, his approach to the gin house is always with fear and trembling. Most frequently they have too little, and therefore it is they are not anxious to leave the field. After winging, follow the whippings; And then the baskets are carried the to the cotton house, and their contents stored away like hay, all hands are being sent in to tramp it down. If the cotton is not dry, instead of taking it to the gin house at once, it is laid upon platforms, two feet high, and some three times as wide, covered with boards or plank, with narrow walks running between them.

This done, the labor of the day is not yet ended, by any means. Each one must then attend his respective chores. One feeds the mules, another the swine-- and other cuts the wood, and so forth; besides, the packing is all done by candlelight. Finally at a late hour, they reached the quarters, sleepy and overcome with the long days toil. Then a fire must be kindled in the cabin, the corn ground in the small handed mill, and supper, and dinner for the next day in the field, prepared. All that is allowed them is corn and bacon, which is given out at the corn crib and smokehouse every Sunday morning. Each one receives, as his weekly allowance, 3 1/2 pounds of bacon, and corn enough up to make a peck of meal. That is all-- no tea, coffee, sugar, and with the exception of of very scanty sprinkling now and then, no salt. I can say, from a 10 years residence with master Epps, that no slave of his is ever likely to suffer from the gout, super induced by excessive high living. Master Epps hogs were fed on shelled corn-- was thrown out to his "niggers" in the ear. The former, he thought, would fatten faster by shelling, and soaking it in the water-- the latter, perhaps, if treated in the same manner, might grow too fat to labor. Master Epps was a shrewd calculator, and knew how to manage his own animals comma drunk or sober.

The corn mill stands in the yard beneath a shelter. It is like a common coffee mill, the hopper holding about 6 quarts. There was one privilege which master Epps granted freely to every slave he had. They might grind their corn nightly, in such small quantities as their daily wants required, or they might grind the whole week's allowance at one time, on Sundays, just as they preferred. A very generous man was master Epps!

I kept my corn in a small wooden box, the meal in a gourd; And, by the way, the cord is one of the most convenient and necessary utensils on a plantation. Besides supplying the place of all kinds of crockery in a slave cabin, it is used for carrying water to the fields. Another, also, contains the dinner. It dispenses with the necessity of pales, dippers, basins, and such tin and wooden superfluities altogether.

When the corn is ground, and fire is made, the bacon is taken down from the nail on which it hangs, a slice cut off and thrown upon the coals to broil. The majority of slaves have no knife, much less a fork. They cut their bacon with the axe at the woodpile. The cornmeal is mixed with a little water, placed in the fire, and baked. When it is "Done brown," The ashes are scraped off, and being placed upon a chip, which answers for a table, the tenant of the slave Hut is ready to sit down upon the ground to supper. By this time it is usually midnight. The same fear of punishment with which they approach the gin-house, Possesses them again on lying down to get a snatch of rest. It is the fear of oversleeping in the morning. Such an offense would certainly be attended with not less than 20 lashes. With a prayer that he may be on his feet and wide awake at the first sound of the horn, he sinks to his slumbers nightly.

The softest couches in the world are not to be found in the log mansion of the slave. The one wherein I reclined year after year, was a plank of 12 inches wide and 10 feet long. My pillow was a stick of wood. The bedding was a coarse blanket, and not a rag or shred beside. Moss might be used, were it not that it directly breeds a swarm of fleas.

The cabin is constructed of logs, without floor or window. The latter is altogether unnecessary, the crevices between the logs admitting sufficient light. In stormy weather the rain drives through them, rendering it comfortless and extremely disagreeable. The rude door hangs on great wooden hinges. In one end is constructed an awkward fireplace.

And hour before daylight the horn is blown. Then the slaves aroused, prepare their breakfast, fill a gourd with water, in another deposit their dinner of cold bacon and corn cake, and hurry to the field again. It is an offence invariably followed by a flogging, to be found at the quarters after daybreak. Then the fears and labours of another day begin; and until its close there is no such thing as rest. He fears he will be caught lagging through the day; he fears to approach the gin house with his basket load of cotton at night; he fears, when he lies down, that he will oversleep himself in the morning. Such is a true, faithful, unexaggerated picture and a description of the slave's daily life, during the time of cotton picking, on the shores of Bayou Boeuf.

9--ALBION

Soon after the Fool's publication of the Regulators' warning and his own reply in " The Verdenton Gazette," he received many letters, some of which may be given as illustrative of the atmosphere in which he lived. The first of these came from a remote portion of the State, and from one of whom the Fool had never even heard :—

" COLONEL COMFORT SERVOSSE. Dear Sir, —I saw your letter in ' The Verdenton Gazette,' and was so struck with the similarity of our positions, that I determined to write to you at once. Some of the worst of our people, as I believe, have formed themselves into a band of Regulators for the sake of attending to everybody's business but their own. I am a native of this State, and fought through the war in the Confederate army, from Bull Run to Appomattox, never missing a day's duty nor a fight. When it was over, I found myself with only a few hundred acres of land (which had been tramped over and burned and stripped by both armies), and no money, no crop, no stock, a large family, some debts, good health, and a constitution like white hickory. I made. up my mind to go to work at once. I went to the nearest post, told my story, and got two horses. I did some hauling, and got some other things, — an army wagon and an ambulance. A friend who happened to have saved some cotton sold it, and loaned me a little money.

I went to work, hired some niggers, told them I would feed them, and work with them, and, when the crop was sold, we would divide. They turned in, and worked. with me. We made a splendid crop, and I divided right smart of money with them in the fall.

" This year some of them wanted to work crops on shares. I could trust them, as they had worked for me the year before. I knew they had enough to bread themselves, and were well able to run a "one-horse crop.' This would allow me to use my means in putting in more land elsewhere, and so be decidedly to my advantage as well as theirs. I was thinking of my own profit, though. when I did it. Well, I sold some of them horses and mules, and helped others to get them elsewhere. The spring opened, and I had the busiest farm and finest prospect I have ever seen. I was running a big force, and every nigger on the plantation had a full crop about half pitched, when all at once I got a notice from the Regulators, just about like the one you publish, only they didn't require me to leave, only to stop selling horses to niggers and letting them crop on shares. They said they had made up their minds that no nigger should straddle his own horse, or ride in his own cart, in this county.

" I saw in a minute that it meant ruin to Exam Davis either way. If I gave in to them, I discouraged my hands. spoilt my crop, and would be swamped by my fertilizer account in the fall. If I didn't, the cussed fools would be deviling and worrying my hands, ham-stringing their stock ,and my crop would be short. It didn't take me long to decide. I made up my mind to fight.

" It wasn't an hour after I read that notice, before I had every horse and mule on the place hauling pine-logs for a stockade ; though I didn't let anybody know what I had on hand. Then I went off to Gainsborough to see the post commander there, Colonel Ricker. He is a good fellow and a gentleman, if he is a Yankee. t told him square out what the matter was ; and he let me have as many old guns as I wanted (part of them surrendered arms, and part extra guns of his command), and a couple boxes of ammunition. When I got back, I told the boys what was up, and distributed the arms. We put our horses in the woods that night, stood to our arms all night, put up the stockade next day, and sent word to the Regulators that they might go to hell. We've kept at work, being mighty careful not to be surprised, and have not been disturbed yet. I don't reckon we shall be; but there is no telling. I say, Stand your ground. They say you're a Yank ; ' but that don't make any difference. Law's law, and right's right; and I hope you will give anybody that comes to disturb you as warm a welcome as they would get here from

" Yours respectfully,

"Exum DAVIS."

The next was from the old doctor, George D. Garnet:—

"MY DEAR COLONEL, —I was sorry to see that the feeling against you, because you are of Northern birth, which has been smol-dering ever since you came among us, has at last burst into a flame. I have been expecting it all the time, and so can not say I am surprised ; but it has been so long in showing itself, that I was truly in hopes that you would escape further molestation. I know that I had no rea-son to anticipate such a result, because you represent a development utterly antagonistic to that in the midst of which you are placed, and are so imbued with its spirit that you can not lay aside nor conceal its characteristics. That civilization by which you are surrounded has never been tolerant of opinions which do not harmonize with its ideas. Based and builded on slavery, the ideas which were a part of that institution, or which were necessary to its protection and development, have become ingrained, and essential to the existence of the community. It was this development which was even more dangerous and inimical to the nation than the institution itself. You must remember, dear Colonel, that neither the nature, habits of thought, nor prejudices of men, are changed by war or its results. The institution of slavery is abolished ; but the prejudice, intolerance, and bitterness which it fostered and nourished, are still alive, and will live until those who were raised beneath its glare have moldered back to dust. A new generation perhaps many new generations — must arise before the North and the South can be one people, or the prejudices, resentments, and ideas of slavery, intensified by unsuccessful war, can be obliterated.

" I hope you will not be discouraged. Your course is the right one, and by pursuing it steadily you will sow the seed of future good. You may not live to reap its advantages, or to see others gather its fair fruits ; but, as God is the God of truth and right he will send a husbandman who will some time gather full sheaves from your seeding, if you do not faint."

The next letter was from a Union man of considerable eminence, who occupied the important position of public prosecutor in the courts of the State. He wrote a letter which is significant in many ways of the public sentiment of the day :

" COLONEL COMFORT SERVOSSE. Dear Sir, --I notice by your letter in The Gazette ' that you are not only angry, but also surprised, at the outrageous demands of the Regulators. Your anger is but natural but your surprise, you will allow me to say, shows an understanding simple and unschooled.'

That you should be unable to measure the strength of prejudice in the Southern mind is not strange. You should remember that the war has rather intensified than diminished the pride, the arrogance, and the sectional rancor and malevolence of the Southern people. If you will consider it for a moment, you will see that this is the natural and unavoidable result of such a struggle. All that made the Southern slaveholder and rebel what he was, still characterizes him since the surrender. The dogma of State-sovereignty has been prevented from receiving practical development, but as a theory it is as vital and as sacred as ever. The fact of slavery is destroyed : the right to enslave is yet as devoutly held as ever. The right of a white man to certain political privileges is admitted : the right of a colored man to such, it will require generations to establish. It is not at you as an individual that the blow struck ; but these people feel that you, by the very fact of Northern birth, and service in the Federal army, represent a' power which has deprived them of property, liberty, and a right to control their own, and that now, in sheer wantonness of insult, you are en-couraging the colored people to do those two things which are more sacred than any other to the Southern mind ; to wit, to buy and hold land and to ride their own horses. You can not understand why they should feel so, because you were never submitted to the same influ-ences. You have a right to be angry ; but your surprise is incredible to them, and pitiable to me.

" To show you to what extent prejudice will extend, permit me to relate an incident yet fresh in my mind. During a recent trial in the court at Martinsville I had occasion to challenge the jurors upon the trial of an indictment of a white man for killing a negro. The Court, after some hesitation, permitted me to ask each juror this question, Have you any feeling which would prevent you from convicting a white man for the murder of a negro, should the evidence show him to be guilty? ' Strange and discreditable as it may appear to you, it be-came necessary, in addition to the regular panel, to order three writs of venire, of fifty each, before twelve men could be found who could answer this simple question in the negative. When prejudice goes so far that 150 men. Acknowledge upon their oaths that they will not convict a white man for killing a negro you must not be surprised that the antebellum dislike and distrust of northern men should show itself in the same manner.

Yours to command,
Thomas Denton

10

10—CORNELIA

Affairs grew steadily worse. All the sheep and cattle were driven away and Yankee soldiers became frequent visitors, spying over the place to see if anything contraband was hidden, taking every shotgun and pistol to be found, leaving no firearms about the place as a protection against marauders, and often roughly demanding that the ladies wardrobes and bureaus be opened for inspection. The ladies did as commanded and looked on with disdain, while the children made faces which so embarrassed one of them he called the search off. Of course it does not seem zealous or courageous to a prejudiced mind to be routed by a few women, but show me the man who has any sort of gallantry that does not succumb before one beautiful woman, and two of these were bewitching damsels, Adelaide and Isabel. They were said to be descended from General Washington's brother Charles and had all the fine bearing of the general, combined with the grace and beauty of several generations of elegant mothers. The officer in question so manifested his dissatisfaction at doing his duty he generously handed his beautiful silver mounted weapon to Mrs. Random when she complained of having nothing to defend the family from undue intrusion. If he ever reads this, he will know that a chivalrous deed is not forgotten. The disdainful girls, even, wished he was on their side. That night some thieves were making encroachments on the chicken roosts when Mrs. Random fired three successive shots, dispersing them-- they throwing themselves across their saddles without taking time to mount, and letting their horses have full reign.

In the household was a northern governess whom the children saw waving to the gunboats when they first appeared, and thinking it a bad sign they, in their enthusiasm, refused to be taught by her any longer. While humoring them in the matter Mrs. Random continued to be courteous and made them so, giving her a pleasant home for some months-- until it was possible for her to go through the lines to the North. She had been in various branches of the family for years, received as one of them, but she never became quite Southernized like many others from the north, and always sent her money to be invested there.

One day two confederate guerrillas came dashing in, following in pursuit of two Federal marauders, and after a few shots exchanged, disarmed the federals and presented their weapons to the ladies of the house. But they were not of much service to the ladies, who were afraid of the enemy finding them in their searches. Not wishing to pay the penalty of having such telltale articles about, they returned them to the captors, thank them for their good intentions, complimented them for their previous prowess in arresting the prowlers, and gave them a good dinner as a reward for saving the chicken roost and other good things the prowlers might have demanded, though the latter got some dinner too.

Once the ladies were subjected to the most unpleasant situation of having a negro guard around the house for a day. They thought this the greatest indignity of all. All persons owning property were compelled to take the oath to save it from being foraged. One French girl made a great to do over it, and proposed getting out of it by reminding the Provost Marshall that she was a lady and could not swear. But in spite of all her protestations the enemy insisted, and she had to swear.

10-- SOLOMON

For some days I was employed at Turner's in repairing his sugar house, When a cane knife was put into my hand, and with 30 or 40 others, I was sent into the field. I found no such difficulty in learning the art of cutting cane that I had in picking cotton. It came to me naturally and intuitively, and in short time I was able to keep up with the fastest knife. Before the cutting was over, however, Judge Tanner transferred me from the field to the sugar house, to act there in the capacity of driver. From the time of the commencement of sugar making to the clothes, the grinding and boiling does not cease day or night. The whip was given me with directions to use it upon anyone who was caught standing idle. If I failed to obey them to the letter, there was another one for my own back. In addition to this my duty was to call on and off the different gangs at the proper time period I had no regular periods of rest, and could never snatch but a few moments of sleep at a time.

It is the custom in Louisiana, as I presume it is in other slave states, to allow the slave to retain whatever compensation he may obtain for services performed on Sundays. In this way, only, are they able to provide themselves with any luxury or convenience whatever. When a slave, purchased, or kidnapped in the north, is transported to a cabin on Bayou Boeuf he is furnished with neither knife, nor fork nor dish, nor kettle, nor any other thing in the shape of crockery, or furniture of any nature or description. He is furnished with a blanket before he reaches there, handed wrapping that around him, he can either stand up, or lie down upon the ground, or on a board, if his master has no use for it. He is at liberty to find a gourd in which to keep his meal, or he can eat his corn from the cob, just as he pleases. To ask the master for a knife, or skillet, or any small convenience of the kind, would be answered with a kick, or laughed at as a joke. Whatever necessary article of this nature is found in a cabin has been purchased with Sunday money. However injurious to the morals, it is certainly a blessing to be the physical condition of the slave, to be permitted to break the Sabbath. Otherwise there would be no way to provide himself with any utensils, which seem to be indispensable to him who is compelled to be his own cook.

On cane plantations in sugar time, there is no distinction as to the days of the week. It is well understood that all hands must labor on the Sabbath, and it is equally well understood that those especially who are hired, as I was to Judge Turner, and others in succeeding years, shall receive remuneration for it. It is usual, also, in the most hurrying time of cotton picking, to require the same extra service. From this source, slaves generally are afforded an opportunity of earning sufficient to purchase a knife, a kettle, tobacco and so forth. The females, discarding the latter luxury, are apt to expend their little revenue in the purchase of gaudy ribbons, wherewithal to deck their hair in in the merry season of the holidays.

I remained in Saint Mary's until the 1st of January, during which time my Sunday money amounted to $10. I met with other good fortune, for which I was indebted to my violin, my constant companion, the source of profit, and soother of my sorrows during years of servitude. There was a grand a party of whites assembled at Mr. Yarney's, in Centreville, a hamlet in the vicinity of Turner's plantation. I was employed to play for them, and so well pleased word the merrymakers with my performance, that a contribution was taken for my benefit, which amounted to $17.00.

With this sum in possession, I was looked upon by my fellows as a millionaire. It afforded me great pleasure to look at it--to count it over and over again, day after day. Visions of cabin furniture, of water pails, of pocket knives, new shoes and coats and hats, floated through my fancy, and up through all rose the triumphant contemplation, that I was the wealthiest "nigger" on Bayou Boeuf.

Vessels run up the Rio Teche to Centreville. While there, I was bold enough One day to present myself before the captain of a steamer, and beg permission to hide myself among the freight. I was emboldened to risk the hazard of such a step, from overhearing a conversation, in the course of which I ascertained he was a native of the north. I did not relate to him the particulars of my history, but only expressed an ardent desire to escape from slavery to a free state. He pitied me, but said it would be impossible to avoid the vigilant custom house officers in New Orleans, and that detection would subject him to punishment, and his vessel to confiscation. My earnest entreaties evidently excited his sympathies, and doubtless he would have yielded to them, could he have done so with any kind of safety. I was compelled to smother the sudden flame that lighted up my bosom with sweet hopes of liberation, and turn my steps once more toward the increasing darkness of despair.

10-- ALBION

" WHAT you tink ob de League, Kunnel ? " said a sturdy, intelligent colored man, who, under direction of Comfort Servosse, was pruning the grape-vines that were scattered about in all manner of unexpected places, as well as in the staid and orderly rows of the vineyard at 'Warrington. It was a bright day in winter; and the stricken soldier was gathering strength and vitality by the unconscious medicament of the soft sunshine and balmy breezes, and that light labor which the care of trees and vines encouraged. He stood now critically surveying a long-neglected " Diana," on which he was about to commence operations, his pruning-knife in his hand, and his shears sticking out from a side-pocket of his overalls. At the next vine was working his interlocutor, who glanced slyly towards him as he asked the question.

" The League,' Andy ? " said Servosse, looking at his co-laborer with an amused smile, while he tried the edge of his knife with his thumb. " What league do you mean? "

" De Union League, ob co'se. Didn't know dar was any udder. Is dar ? " said Andy, as he finished tying up the vine at which he had been at work, and started to the next.

" Oh, yes ! there are various kinds of leagues. But why do you inquire about the Union League ? How did you ever here of it ? "

" Wal, putty much de same way you did, I 'spects," answered Andy with a grin.

" Pretty much as I did? " said Servosse. " What do you mean?"

" Why, I 'llow you b'longs to it," said Andy. " Dey tells me every Union soldier b'longs to it. 'Sides dat, I made de knocks de udder day on de work-bench, when you was workin' at de wisteria in front o' de winder, an' I seed you look up kinder sudden-like, an' den smile to youself as if you thought you'd heerd from an ole friend, an' woke up to find ye'd been a-dreamin'."

" So I did, Andy," answered the Caucasian. " Some time during the war I heard of an organization known as the Union League. It strikes me that I first heard of it in the mountains of East Tennessee, as instituted for self-protection and mutual support among the sturdy Unioners there in those trying times. However that may be, I first came in contact with its workings in the fall of 1864. It was the very darkest period of the war for us. The struggle had lasted so long that everybody was tired out. The party in the North who were opposed to the war " —

" Wasn't they called ' Copperheads ' ? " interrupted Andy.

" Yes, we called them Copperheads,' " answered the Fool. " These men seemed to think that it would be a good time to stop the war, on the idea that both sides were tired of it, and would rather end it on any terms than keep it up on uncertainties. So they were making great efforts to elect a president who would let up on the Rebellion, and enable the rebels of the South to accomplish their secession. At this time I escaped from a Confederate prison, and after a time arrived in Philadelphia. While I waited there for orders, a friend asked me one night if I didn't want to join the Union League. Upon asking what it was, I found that it was a society of men who were determined never to give up the Union under any hazard, but to uphold and sustain it with property and_life if need be. It was a secret association; and its chief purpose was said to be to enable the loyal people of any city or neighborhood to muster at the shortest possible notice, to resist invasion, put down riot, or enforce the law,—to protect themselves and families, or aid the government in extremities."

" Was it any good?" asked Andy.'

" Well, indeed," responded his employer musingly, "I do not know. A soldier who was on duty at the front the greater part of the war had very little opportunity for knowing what went on at the rear. I have heard that when 'Lee marched over the mountain-wall ' into Maryland 'and Pennsylvania, and threatened Philadelphia and Baltimore, the bells of Philadelphia struck the signals of the League, and thousands rallied at their places of assembly in an instant; and that regiment after regiment of resolute minute-men were organized and equipped almost without an hour's delay. I know nothing about it."

" Do you want dis Concord ' cut back to two eyes, like de rest, Kunnel? It's made a powerful strong growth, an' it seems a clar waste to cut it back so close," asked the hireling, as he held up for his employer's inspection a rank-grown cane of the previous year, which had run along the ground until it had appropriated the stake of a weakling neighbor, and clambered over it, smothering in its sturdy coils the growth of the rightful owner.

" Yes," said Servosse hesitatingly, "cut it down. It seems a pity, as you say, to destroy that beautiful growth ; but, when vines have run wild for a time, the only way to bring them back to sober, profitable bearing, is to cut them back without scruple. Cut them down to two eyes, if they are as big as your wrist, Andy. It's wasting the past, but saving the future. And it's my notion that the same thing is true of peoples and nations, Andy. For instance, when a part of a country rebels, and runs wild for a time, it ought to have the rank wood, the wild growth, cut away without mercy. They ought to be held down, and pruned and shaped, until they are content to bear the peaceable fruits of righteousness,' instead of. clambering about, 'cumbering the ground' with a useless growth."

" You was sayin' what de League had done, a while ago," said Andy, after there had been a period of silence, while they each cut away at their respective vines.

" Yes," said Servosse. "I have heard, too, that the order was very useful as a sort of reserve force in the rear, in putting down such terrible riots as were gotten up in New York in the dark days of the war, by emissaries of the enemy, acting with the Copperheads of the North."

" Was dar many of 'ern— de Leaguers I mean ? " asked Andy.

"I understand," was the reply, "that it spread pretty much all through the North in the later years of the war, and embraced a very large portion of the Union men in those States."

"Did all de Yankee soldiers belong to it ? " queried the listener.

"Really, I don't know," said Servosse. " I don't suppose I have ever heard more than a dozen or two say anything about it in the army. I suppose most of the veterans who went home on leave of absence in 1864 may have joined it while at home, and the new levies may have belonged to it. Of course, we had no need for such an organization in the army."

" Well, is der any harm in it, Kunnel? Any reason why any body shouldn't jine it? " asked Andy earnestly.

" None in the world, that I can see," answered Servosse. "Indeed, I do not see why it should not be a good thing for the colored people to do. It would teach them to organize and work together, and they would learn in it something about those public duties which are sure very soon to be cast upon them. Besides, it is by no means sure that they may not need it as a means of self-protection. I had not thought of it before; but I believe it might be a good thing."

" Dat's my notion, Mars' Kunnel. We's got a little league down h'yer to Verdenton at de schoolhouse fer de culled folks, an' we'd be mighty proud to hey ye come down some Chuseday night. Dat we would ! " said Andy.

" What ! you have got a chapter of the Union League there? "

" Yes : it's jes' like what you's been a-tellin"bout."

" How did you get it? "

" Wal, I don't jes' 'zactly know. Dar's some culled men belongs to it as was soldiers in de Union army, an' I 'llowed dey might hey fotch it wid 'em when dey come h'yer. Data what made me ax you so close 'bout dat."

" Who belong to it? Are they all colored members? "

"Wal, de heft ob 'em is culled, ob co'se; but der's a right smart sprinklin' ob white folks, arter all.

Editor--As is often the case in time of war, not all men were eager to join the military. Both the Union and Confederacy conscripted men for service. Doing so could be problematic. There was no Selective Service, no national database of eligible young men. As was generally the case in these times, conscription was a local affair. Now, following the war, a conversation takes place concerning Union sympathizers in the South, and how they avoided being conscripted into the Confederate army. A young 'draft dodger' named Durfee has met Comfort and introduces him to another draft dodger, a Mr. Walters. Some ways to avoid the draft were to hold elected office, have a government contract to supply goods, or to simply hide out. Mr. Walters had done none of these.

" Mr. Walters," said Durfee, "was one of our staunchest Union men. I knew him all through the war. Strangely enough, he did not hide out, nor hold an office, nor take a contract."

" How in the word did you keep out of the army? " asked Servosse.

" I hardly know," answered Walters ,pleasantly. " I think it was my health mainly."

" Ha, ha, ha ! " broke in Durfee. " Your health, did you say? I vow I b'leve you're right. — He had better health, and more of it, during the war, than any man I know of, colonel."

" I don't understand how he kept out, then," said Servosse.

" There ain't anybody that I ever met that does understand it," said Durfee. " He was living in Rockford when the war began, in business, making money, and a member of the Methodist Church. He wanted to go away at the first ; but his wife said she didn't want to leave her people: so John Walters staid right where he was, and went on trading, and minding his own business, the same as before. After a while, when things begun to get hot, there was some talk among the town loafers about his going to the army. Then he spoke out, and said that he was a Union man, and didn't never calculate to be any thing else.

He shouldn't do any fighting against the government willingly, and they'd better not try to make him do it unwillingly. Things kep' gittin' hotter an' hotter ; the conscript laws kep' growing closer an' closer : but John Walters was right there in Rockford, a-tradin' an' tendin' to his own business, the same as ever. A good deal was said about it ; because he was just the same Union man as ever, never saying any thing about the matter unless tackled on it, and then giving as good as was sent. It got noised around somehow that he had said, that, if he was compelled to go, the man whom he thought at the bot tom of it would be in some danger. He wasn't no man to trifle with, and so he went on unmolested. Finally a young conscript officer came to the town, and talked pretty loud about what he would do. Some things he said came to Walters's ears; and he went over to see him, carryin' a walking-stick in his hand. They met on the porch. I never knew what passed ; but a man who saw it told me that the officer drew his pistol, an' another man caught Walters's right arm. I don't reckon anybody knows just how it was done, —not even Walters himself. They were all there in a crowd; but when it broke up Walters had the pistol, the officer had a bullet somewhere through his jaw, another man had a broken arm, and another had somehow tumbled off the porch and sprained his foot, so that he could not walk for a month. Walters was the only one unhurt. He reported here next day ; was examined by a medical board, and somehow pronounced unfit for duty. He went home a few days afterwards with his exemption-papers all in due form, and in fact they never did get him. Of course, he was prosecuted and bedeviled ; but when the war over there was was John Walters, --just where he was when it begun."

" That is a very unusual experience, Mr. Walters," said the colonel, turning towards him as Durfee concluded.

" Yes," said Walters modestly : "I was very fortunate. I looked poorly, as I always have, and I did not 'push myself into difficulty. They knew if I went that I would desert, and go into the Union lines the first chance I got: so there was no use of sending me to the front. But I had a much easier time than Durfee or a half-dozen others here. Why, there is a man, Colonel, who lived in an excavation under his house for eighteen months. There is another who staid for five months under a cedar-tree which grew all alone on the top of a hill within two hundred yards of the big road. There's two others who were of a party of seven who hid from the conscript hunters in a cave on Martin Holbrook's laud, which they dug out of the side of a creek, and up into the bank above, when the water was out of the pond. When the gate was shut down, and the water rose, they had to dive like otters to get into their bole."

Editor--Later, Servosse asks an acquaintance what he knows of the Union League. Mr. Walters was a Southerner, but had been a Union man during the civil war. Efforts by the Confederates to draft him went badly, for the Confederates.

"Is the League organized to any great extent in the South ? asked Comfort.

"I don't know," responded Walters. " Just before the close of the war, I went up into East Tennessee on a little business that took me through the lines, and I joined it there. I don't like it."

"Why not ? "

"It's too cumbrous. Our people ain't educated enough to run it well.. Besides that, I don't like these big meetings."

" But is it not an educator for the colored men`? "

"I've thought of that, and it's the great redeeming feature of the institution. I'm thinking we shall need something more practical, and that don't make so much show, before we have done with the matters rising out of the war."

" You do not take a hopeful view of the future, then?"

" Well, that depends altogether on the view of the present that the government and the Northern people take. if they get the notion that rebellion has transformed those engaged in it into sanctified and glorified saints, as they seem in a way to do, why, the war will not amount to any certain sum, so far as liberty and progress are concerned. Then

Union men an' niggers will have to hunt- their holes, and will be worse off in fact than they were during the war. I'm 'fraid it's going to be so, Colonel ; and I feel as if I ought to go to the West, where I and my children can be free and safe."

" I hope you will not think of that, Mr. Walters," said the Fool.

" Well, I have thought of it strongly ; but I have decided to stay," was the reply, " chiefly because so many of you Northern men have come down here. I think, that, if you can stand it, I can. At least, I don't think we native Unionists ought to run away, and leave you."

" You were speaking about the president," said Comfort suggestively.

" Well," laughed Walters, " I didn't mean that there was any danger in him. He was every thing to all men during the war, and will be any thing to anybody until the end of time, if it will butter bread for Tommy. Sanderson."

11

11-- CORNELIA

When the war was over, the slaves freed, and all the preliminaries of peace gone through with, there was nothing observed to demonstrate the fact in the remote parts of Texas--nor anyone around to enforce it-- and one day when Mr. Random was sitting on the porch of his log cabin smoking his pipe, bemoaning his losses, and thinking how the sudden freedom of his slaves would have a tendency to narrow his already depleted purse, a man from Cuba, Don Antonio Daselio, whose acquaintance he had previously made, appeared in the gate, making a low bow as is the custom with Spaniards.

Mr. Random rose to greet him, giving him a cordial shake of the hand, and begged him to be seated. When he had settled himself in a comfortable rocker and discourse on the weather and minor topics a little he said:

"So, Mr. random, the war is over."

"Yes, and I'll be glad to get home."

"What will you do with the niggers Mr. random?"

"Take them along, too"

"Sacre! Whew! What great expense! What sacrefeece!" (Daseelio, like many foreigners, lapsed into broken English when he was excited or off his guard.) "De nigger he is happier when he slave, happier dan in Afrique--I give you $200,000 for dem, Mr. Random. Nigger die if he free, nigger no know how to take care of himself, nigger surely die, Mr. Random. Your kindness is meestaken, Sir, meestaken. I give you de money in gold, Sir, in gold, cash, sir."

Mr. random went on smoking his pipe, which had gone out and been relighted during the conversation, looked at the Don out of the corners of his eyes to see if he could discover any indications of insanity, and remarked quietly:

"Negroes are of no value now, Don; You must be joking."

"Yes, yes, dey are-- dey are in Cuba. I ship dem there. Just sell 'em. I'll take the responsibilitee. You pay for de nigger, you never stole him, you have right to get your money back."

"How much did you say?"

"$200,000 tousand dollar gold, cash."

"That's a big sum these hard times, Don."

"Yes, and you go home and feex up your place wid de money and lib lak a preence—on de odder hand you may struggle for years and never be reech."

"Well, Don, your offer is tempting. I was thinking just of such things when I saw you enter; take dinner with me, and I will see what I can do for you," which so elated the Don he did not notice the brown study his host was in the while.

After dinner Mr. Random had the darkies assembled and presented them to the Don, told them the issues of the war, the offer of the Don (whose eyes were sparkling), and before their dazed minds could plunge from the hope of freedom to the abyss of Cuban captivity--or were even able to recognize the magnanimity of his character, he told the Cuban he had never broken his word to any man, that he must abide by the decision of the war, as he had told them he would—that he would not sell them. For a moment there was silence. Then a great shout arose. The sturdiest men of the dusky group took the master on their shoulders and paraded him around, with wild songs of happiness, and gave themselves a grand jubilee. Even the Don's eyes were misty, and he joined in the shout. Much of our unkindness to others is a lack of knowing their heart's desires rather than direct cruelty, and it was not long before Mr. Random left for Louisiana with those negroes who wished it.

After his return he reinstated himself upon his plantations, hoping in a few years, with care and economy, to be fairly comfortable.

All the people of Louisiana, after the war, taking heart from the fact that they had a better outlook than those in the States which were more the seat of war and devastation, got what they could together and started afresh. At the country stores, on the steamboats, and wherever it was convenient to gather, the conversation always drifted to the war and the changes it had wrought.

At the White Castle, ever an interesting center, the family associates and their guests assembled and related their various experiences around the winter hearth.

One evening in the early fall, following the war, the family, including some friends, were in the library, according to their usual custom ; Adelaide and Isabel sitting comfortably about with their shapely heads resting against the big chair backs, Penelope and Eugenia giggling in one corner, Bertha playing with some cats on the hearthrug, Richard reading near by, and Patricia with some embroidery in hand. Algernon and the older people, including Mr. and Mrs. Random, an elderly neighbor, Mrs. Hastings, a Mrs. Johnston from New Orleans, and the boys' former tutor, all seated in rocking-chairs before the crackling fire—for the Randoms burned wood in the library. The tutor was relating his war experiences. He was originally from Pennsylvania, was rather quick-tempered in school, for he thought nothing of catching the boys by the collar and shaking them against the wall when he got out of patience—so it was whispered among themselves.

He was too conscientious. He kept the boys in on the slightest provocation, they thought. Old Dan, who drove the dogcart every afternoon for a neighbor's boys, would get so tired waiting he would say: " Dat teacher might's well let 'em go, 'tain gwine do no good, nohow." And subsequent events seemed to verify that statement in regard to Dan's young masters. But the tutor loved the South so well he fought and suffered for it, and I believe the boys forgave him his shortcomings in the schoolroom when they heard of his hairbreadth escapes in behalf of the Cause.

Through friends he made during the war he became very prosperous, when he afterward went into business in Memphis, Tennessee.

11--SOLOMON

The only respite from constant labor the slave has through the whole year, is during the Christmas holidays. Epps allowed us three--others allow four, five and six days, according to the measure of their generosity. It is the only time to which they look forward with any interest or pleasure. They are glad when night comes, not only because it brings them a few hours repose, but because it brings them one day nearer Christmas. It is hailed with equal delight by the old and the young; even Uncle Abram ceases to glorify Andrew Jackson, and Patsy forgets her many sorrows, amid the general hilarity of the holidays. It is the time of feasting, and frolicking, and fiddling--The carnival season with the children of bondage. They are the only days when they are allowed a little restricted liberty, and heartily indeed do they enjoy it.

It is the custom for one planter to give a" Christmas supper," inviting the slaves from neighboring plantations to join his own on the occasion; for instance, one year it is given by Epps, the next by Marshall, the next by Hawkins, and so on. Usually from 3 to 500 are assembled, coming together on foot, in carts, on horseback, on mules, riding double and triple, sometimes a boy and girl, at others a girl and two boys, and at others again a boy, a girl and an old woman. Uncle Abram astride a mule, with Aunt Phebe and Patsy behind him, trotting towards a Christmas supper, would be no uncommon sight on Bayou booth.

Then, two, "of all days i' the year," they array themselves in their best attire. The cotton coat has been washed clean, the stump of a tallow candle has been applied to the shoes, and if so fortunate as to possess a rimless or crownless hat, it is placed jauntily on the head. They are welcomed with equal cordiality, however, if they come a bare-headed and barefooted to the feast. As a general thing, the women wear handkerchiefs tied around their heads, but if chance has thrown in their way a fiery red ribbon, or a cast off bonnet of their mistress' grandmother, it is sure to be worn on such occasions. Red--the deep blood of red--is decidedly the favorite color among the enslaved damsels of my acquaintance. If a red ribbon does not encircle the neck, you will be certain to find all the hair of their woolly heads tied up with the red strings of one sort or another.

The table is spread in the open air, handle loaded with varieties of meat and piles of vegetables. Bacon and cornmeal at such times are dispensed with. Sometimes the cooking is performed in the kitchen on the plantation, and others in the shade of wide branching trees. In the latter case, a ditch is dug in the ground, and wood laid in and burned until it is filled with glowing coals, over which chickens, ducks, turkeys, and pigs, and not unfrequently the entire body of a wild ox, are roasted. They are furnished also with flour, of which biscuits are made, and often with Peach and other preserves, with tarts, and every manner and description of pies, except the mince, that being an article of pastry as yet unknown among them. Only the slave who has lived all the years on the scanty allowance of meal and bacon, can appreciate such suppers. White people in great numbers assemble to witness the gastronomical enjoyments.

They seat themselves at the rustic table--the males on one side, the females on the other. The two Between whom there may have been an exchange of tenderness, invariably managed to sit opposite; for the omnipresent Cupid disdains not to hurl his arrows into the simple hearts of slaves unalloyed and exalting happiness lights up the dark faces of them all. The ivory teeth, contrasting with their black complexions, exhibit 2 long, white streaks the whole extent of the table. All round the bountiful board a multitude of eyes roll in ecstasy. Giggling and laughter and the clattering of cutlery and crockery succeed. Cufee's elbow hunches his neighbors side, impelled by an involuntary impulse of delight; Nelly shakes her finger at sambo and last, and she knows not why, and so the fun and merriment flows on.

Alas! had it not been for my beloved violin, I scarcely can conceive how I could have endured the long years of bondage. It introduced me to great houses--relieved me of many days labor in the field-- supplied me with conveniences for my cabin-- with pipes and tobacco, and extra pairs of shoes, and oftentimes led me away from the presence of a hard master, to witness scenes of jollity and mirth. It was my companion--the friend of my bosom--triumphing loudly when I was joyful, and uttering its soft, melodious consolations when I was sad. Often, at midnight, when sleep had fled affrighted from the cabin, and my soul was disturbed and troubled with the contemplation of my fate, it would sing me a song of peace. On the holy Sabbath days, when an hour or two of leisure was allowed, it would accompany me to some quieter place on the Bayou bank, and, lifting up its voice, discourse kindly and pleasantly indeed. It heralded my name around the country--made me friends, who, otherwise would not have noticed me--gave me an honored seat at the yearly feasts, and secured the loudest and heartiest welcome of them all at the Christmas dance. The Christmas dance! Oh, ye pleasure seeking sons and daughters of idleness, who move with measured step, listless and snail like, through the slow winding cotillion, if you wish to look upon the celerity, if not the "poetry of motion"--upon genuine happiness, rampant and unrestrained--go down to Louisiana, and see the slaves dancing in the starlight of a Christmas night.

Marriage is frequently contracted during the holidays, if such an institution may be said to exist among them. The only ceremony required before entering into that "holy estate," Is to obtain the consent of the respective owners. It is usually encouraged by the masters of female slaves. Either party can have as many husbands or wives as the owner will permit, and either is at liberty to discard the other at pleasure. The law in relation to divorce, or to bigamy, and so forth, is not applicable to property, of course. If the wife does not belong on the same plantation with the husband, the latter is permitted to visit her on Saturday nights, if the distance is not too far. Uncle Abrams wife lived 7 miles from Epps, on Bayou Huff Power. He had permission to visit her once a fortnight, but he was growing old, as has been said, and truth to say, he had a latterly well nigh forgotten her. Uncle Abram had no time to spare from his meditations on General Jackson--connubial dalliance being well enough for the young and thoughtless, but unbecoming a grave and solemn philosopher like himself.

The year 1850, down to which time I have now arrived, omitting many occurrences uninteresting to the reader, was an unlucky year for my companion Wiley, the husband of Phebe, whose taciturn and retiring nature has thus far kept him in the background. Notwithstanding Wiley seldom opened his mouth, and revolved in his obscure and unpretending orbit without a grumble, nevertheless the warm elements of sociology were strong in the bosom of that silent "nigger." In the exuberance of his self-reliance, disregarding the philosophy of Uncle Abram, and setting the councils of aunt Phebe utterly at naught, he had the full hardiness to essay a nocturnal visit to a neighboring cabin without a pass.

So attractive was the society in which he found himself, that Wiley took little note of the passing hours, and the light began to break in the east before he was aware. Speeding homeward as fast as he could run, he hoped to reach the quarters before the horn would sound; but, unhappily, he was spied on the way by a company of patrollers.

How it is in other dark places of slavery, I do not know, but on Bayou Boeuf there is an organization of patrollers, as they are styled, whose business it is to seize and whip any slave they may find wondering from the plantation. They ride on horseback, headed by a captain, armed, and accompanied by dogs. They have the right, either by law, or by general consent, to inflict discretionary chastisement upon a black man caught beyond the boundaries of his master's estate without a pass, and even to shoot him, if he attempts to escape. Each company has a certain distance to ride up and down the bayou. They are compensated by the planters, who contribute in proportion to the number of slaves they own. The clatter of their horses hooves dashing by can be heard at all hours of the night, and frequently they may be seen driving a slave before them, or leading him by a rope fastened around his neck, to his owner's plantation.

Wiley fled before one of these companies, thinking he could reach his cabin before they could overtake him; but one of their dogs, a great ravenous hound, gripped him by the leg, and held him fast. The patrollers whipped him severely, and brought him, a prisoner, to Epps. From him he received another flagellation still more severe, so that the cuts of the lash and the bites of the dog rendered him sore, stiff and miserable, insomuch as he was scarcely able to move. It was impossible in such a state to keep up his row and consequently there was not an hour in the day but Wiley felt the sting of his master's rawhide on his raw and bleeding back. His sufferings became intolerable, and finally he resolved to run away. Without disclosing his intentions to run away even to his wife Phebe, he proceeded to make arrangements for carrying his plan into execution. Having cooked his whole week's allowance, he cautiously left the cabin on a Sunday night, after the inmates of the quarters were asleep. When the horn sounded in the morning, Wiley did not make his appearance. Search was made for him in the cabins, in the corn crib, in the cotton house, and in every nook and corner of the premises. Each of us was examined, touching any knowledge we might have that could throw light upon his sudden disappearance or present whereabouts. Epps raved and stormed, and mounting his horse, galloped to neighboring plantations, making inquiries in all directions. The search was fruitless. Nothing whatever was elicited, going to show what had become of the missing man. The dogs were led to the swamp, but were unable to strike his trail. They would circle away through the forest, their noses to the ground, but invariably returned in a short time to the spot from whence started.

Wiley had escaped, and so secretly and cautiously as to elude and baffle all pursuit. Days and even weeks passed away, and nothing could be heard of him. Epps did nothing but curse and swear. It was the only topic of conversation among us when alone. We indulged in a great deal of speculation in regard to him, one suggesting he might have been drowned in some bayou, Inasmuch as he was a poor swimmer; another, that perhaps he might have been devoured by alligators, or stung by the venomous moccasin, whose bite is certain and sudden death. The warm and hearty sympathies of us all, however, were with poor Wiley, wherever he might be. Many an earnest prayer ascended from the lips of Uncle Abram, beseeching safety for the wanderer. In about 3 weeks, when all hope of ever seeing him again was dismissed, to our surprise, he one day appeared among us. While leaving the plantation, he informed us, it was his intention to make his way back to South Carolina--to the old quarters of Master Buford. During the day he remained secreted, sometimes in the branches of a tree, and at night pressed forward through the swamps. Finally, one morning, just at dawn, he reached the shore of Red River. While standing on the bank, considering how he could cross it, a white man accosted him, and demanded a pass. Without one, and evidently a runaway, he was taken to Alexandria, the Shire town of the parish of Rapides, and confined in prison. It happened several days after that Joseph B Roberts, uncle of mistress Epps, was in Alexandria, and going into the jail, recognized him. Wiley had worked on his plantation, when Epps resided at Huff Power. Paying the jail fee, and writing him a pass, underneath which was a note to Epps, requesting him not to whip him on his return, Wiley was sent back to Bayou Boeuf. It was the hope that hung upon this request, and which Roberts assured him would be respected by his master, that sustained him as he approached the house. The request, however, as may be readily supposed, was entirely disregarded. After being kept in suspense 3 days, Wiley was stripped, and compelled to endure one of those inhuman floggings to which the poor slave is so often subjected. It was the first and last attempt of Wiley to run away. The long scars upon his back, which he will carry with him to the grave, perpetually remind him of the dangers of such a step.

11-- ALBION

WHAT is called the period of " Reconstruction " came at last; and in tracing our Fool's story it will be necessary to give some brief attention to this era of our nation's history. It is a short story as one reads it now. Its facts are few and plain. There is no escape from them. They were graven on the hearts of millions with a burning stylus. Short as is the story, it is full of folly and of shame. Regarded with whatever charity, folly and cowardice appear as its chief elements ; and it has already borne too bitter a harvest of crime to believe that the future holds enough of good springing from its gloom to make it ever tolerable to the historian. Let us as briefly as possible retrace its essential features.

At the close of the great war of the Rebellion these conditions presented themselves to the statesmen of the land: — the hostile army was dispersed ; the opposing governmental forms were disrupted ; the Confederacy had set in a night which was declared to be eternal, and its component elements — the subordinate governments or states of which it had been composed — were dissolved.

The North, that portion of the country which for four years had constituted alone the United States of America, was full of rejoicing and gladness, which even the death of its martyr President could not long repress. Sorrow for the dead was lost in joy for the living. Banners waved; drums beat; and the quick step of homeward-marching columns echoed through every corner of the land. The clamor of rejoicing drowned the sighs of those who wept for their unreturning dead. All was light and joy, and happy, peaceful anticipation. The soldier had no need to beat his spear into a plowshare, or his sword into a pruning-hook. He found the plow waiting for him in the furrow. Smiling, peaceful homes, full of plenty and comfort, invited him to new exertion; and the prospect of rich returns for his labor enabled him all the more easily to forgive and forget, to let bygones be bygones, and throwing away the laurels, and forgetting the struggles and lessons of the past, contentedly grow fat on the abundance of the present and the glowing promise of the future.

At the South it was far different. Sadness and gloom covered the face of the land. The returning braves brought no joy to the loving hearts who had sent them forth. Nay, their very presence kept alive the chagrin of defeat. Instead of banners and music and gay greeting, silence and tears were their welcome home. Not only for the dead were these lamentations, but also for the living. If the past was sorrowful, the future was scarcely less so. If that which went before was embittered by disappointment and the memory of vain sacrifice, that which was to come was darkened with uncertainty and apprehension. The good things of the past were apples of Sodom in the hand of the present. The miser's money was as dust of the highway in value; the obligor, in his indefinite promise to pay, had vanished, and the hoarder only had a gray piece of paper stamped with the fair pledge of a ghostly nation. The planter's slaves had become freedmen while he was growing into a hero, and no longer owed fealty or service to him or his family. The home where he had lived in luxury was almost barren of necessities : even the ordinary comforts of life were wanting at his fireside. A piece of cornbread, with a glass of milk, and bit of bacon, was, perhaps, the richest welcome-feast that wifely love could devise for the returning hero. Time and the scath of war had wrought ruin in his home. The hedgerows were upgrown, and the ditches stopped. Those whom he had been wont to see in .delicate array were clad in homespun. His loved ones who had been reared in luxury were living in poverty. While he had fought, interest had run. War had not extinguished debt. What was a mere bagatelle when slaves and stocks were at their highest was a terrible incubus when slaves were no more, and banks were broken. The army of creditors was even more terrible than the army with banners, to whom he had surrendered. If the past was dark, the future was Cimmerian. Shame and defeat were behind, gloom and apprehension before.

Here and there throughout the subjugated land were detachments and posts of the victorious army, gradually growing smaller and fewer as the months slipped by. The forerunners of trade appeared before the smoke of battle had fairly cleared away. After a little, groups of Northern men settled, to engage in commerce, or to till the soil. The cotton and tobacco which
remained of the slender crops of the years of war brought fabulous prices. The hope of their continuance was the one bright spot in the future.

The freedmen, dazed with new-found liberty, crowded the towns and camps, or wandered aimlessly here and there. Hardly poorer than their late masters, they were better prepared for poverty. They had been indurated to want, exposure, and toil. Slavery had been a hard school ; but in it they had learned more than one lesson which was valuable to them now. They could endure the present better than their old masters' families, and had never learned to dread the future.

So a part of the re-united country was in light, and the other part in darkness, and between the two was a zone of bloody graves.

The question for the wise was : How shall this be made light, without darkening that? Not an easy question for the wisest and bravest ; one which was sure of no solution, or only the ill one of chance or mischance, as the Fates might direct, at the hands of vanity, folly, and ambition.

For two years there were indecision and bickering and cross-purposes and false promises. The South waited sullenly the North wonderingly.

So it must have been well understood by the wise men who devised this short-sighted plan of electing a President beyond a peradventure of defeat, that they were giving the power of the reorganized, subordinate republics, into the hands of a race unskilled in public affairs, poor to a degree hardly to be matched in the civilized world, and so ignorant that not five out of a hundred of its voters could read their own ballots, joined with such Adullamites among the native whites as might be willing to face a proscription which would shut the house of God in the face of their families, together with the few men of Northern birth, resident in that section since the close of the war, — either knaves or fools, or partaking of the nature of both, — who might elect to become permanent citizens, and join in the movement.

Against them was to be pitted the wealth, the intelligence, the organizing skill, the pride, and the hate of a people whom it had taken four years to conquer in open fight when their enemies outnumbered them three to one, who were animated chiefly by the apprehension of what seemed now about to be forced upon them by this miscalled measure of " Reconstruction ; " to wit, the equality of the negro race.

It was done, too, in the face of the fact that within the preceding twelvemonth the white people of the South, by their representatives in the various Legislatures of the Johnsonian period, had absolutely refused to recognize this equality, even in the slightest matters, by refusing to allow the colored people to testify in courts of justice against white men, or to protect their rights of person and property in any manner from the avarice, lust, or brutality of their white neighbors. It was done in the very face of the " Black Codes," which were the first in active moments of provisional legislatures, and which would have established a serfdom more complete than that of the Russian steppes before the rise of Alexander.

12

12—CORNELIA

Editor—Family and friends are gathered at the White Castle. Some recite poetry that has been written relative to the civil war. Below are two stanzas and chorus from The Conscript:

It is true that all young ladies say. To war you'd better go,

But then I find they're very glad to have me for a beau.

They say that when this war is over, a soldier lad will be

The only one to get a wife; but wait a while, you'll see.

And there are several minor things, my darkies and my crop,

My house and the land, my own dear self, and everything I've got.

And if I go, all these are lost. Then is it, right to go?

And camp is such a horrid place, and I love my comfort. So.

Hurrah! Hurrah!

I know what I shall do.

I'll save my own dear, precious self.

And let my country go!

This caused unusual mirth. Finally Mr. Bagnell, his daughter Miranda and son John, a few years older than Penelope, were announced by Penelope and Eugenia, who, it seemed, liked to go to the door in the evenings, which was all very well, for the servants wished to be dismissed as soon as tea was over, after the war. Mr. Bagnell and Miranda shook hands all around, Miranda taking a seat near Adelaide and Isabel, whom Algernon joined; Mr. Bagnell, as usual, sitting or standing where he could best be seen and heard, and they both immediately asked Leo all manner of questions concerning his campaign. John went with Richard and the little girls, Penelope and Eugenia.

Leo had heard of Miranda's daring, and in his turn inquired of her jokingly how she had kept the Yankees " from appropriating her pa's molasses."

" Oh, that was easy enough. When I saw the gunboat about to land I thought they (meaning the Federals) were coming after the molasses on the levee waiting to be shipped, and I went out with my pistol, which I usually had about me in those days. Jumping on the first row of barrels, I told the men who came off for the purpose to touch them at the peril of their lives, and they didn't do it either," she said with flashing eyes.

Of course this announcement would have startled a stranger, but Miranda was naturally brave, and having this quality strengthened by her helpless position when her father was off to the war, none of the company were surprised, but rather applauded her spirit.

Mr. Bagnell now said: " This is all very amusing, but I can tell you some heartrending circumstances which happened in Virginia."

The young people listened and caught the intense feelings that were wrenching the hearts of the elders and treasured them in their memories. He went on to tell of a noble old gentleman whom Mr. Random knew-well, and who returning when the enemy had retreated after a fight around his cherished home, found the fences leveled and burned, the shade trees cut down in his yard, the fruit trees barked by their horses as far as they could reach, the gravestones of his loved ones defaced and broken—every evidence of wanton destruction, while in the house the furniture was hacked by axes, the feathers in the beds and pillows scattered on the floors, lard thrown all over them from his storeroom, the family portraits slashed and punctured.

While viewing these evidences of fanaticism, looking into his parlor, where had been an old Colonial mantel, and its over-mirror now lying on the hearth in fragments, he heard a groan, and straining his old eyes discovered a Yankee soldier, wounded and left alone, prone upon his back.

Approaching nearer, he heard him faintly pleading for water. Turning and glancing around on the scene of destruction, he left him, found a vessel, descended the long hill to the spring to bring back the first bucket of water he ever carried in his life, knelt by the side of the enemy, raised his head, placed the fresh water to his lips, and said : " God forgive you." As the sun was dropping behind the Peaks of Otter that evening, with such aid as he could summon, he wrapped the dead soldier in his U. S. blanket and buried him in the corner of his garden.

Mr. Random said it was a hard situation to be placed in, and that it was the right course to have pursued, but how few would have done it, and that he was a veritable apple of gold, one with the utmost polish.

" Yes, yes," said Mr. Bagnell, shaking his head, his remarks taking a wider range. " The Yankees forced the war on us and have set the negroes free, breaking up an institution with much concrete good to redeem it, thereby creating a more complex problem, with no reason in its defense, only an abstract theory founded on a false premise of equality, at the cost and sacrifice of so many and better lives that the whole negro race can never redeem the debt."

" Though I do not think," said Mr. Random, " negroes and whites will ever be equal, socially, I do not think war is right, nor do I fully approve of slavery, though it has been the means of elevating and Christianizing savages in a degree, but I think a great injustice has been done us by giving this hoard of ignorant people absolute freedom, depriving us of our vested rights without any sort of compensation, with old and helpless negroes on our hands to be cared for. I think, like John J. Crittenden, arbitration would have been much better than all this mad sacrifice of life and treasure, but this is not the first time in the world's history great wrongs have been done in the name of liberty, and our duty now is to go forward and do what we can to bring order out of the chaos which surrounds us, my friend."

Mr. Bagnell was so eager to speak he could hardly wait for Mr. Random to finish, and as was his habit when excited, he rose from his chair and walked around the room.

" Why, Random! you do not believe in war, you? When you let your slaves build railroads and dig nitre for the cause, while you might have raised cotton and sold it at fabulous prices over the border. You do not believe in war?"

" Well, Bagnell, I don't, but I had to be loyal to the South, and do not regret it. I have ever been for peace and did not think secession would help us—but I did hope to thrash the Yankees, as long as they brought us into it, and go back into the Union of our own accord."

" Well said ! Well said ! I think better of you, indeed I do. Good night. Come on, Miranda," and with a flourish of his cane he always carried at night he bowed himself out with Miranda in the wake, the latter laughing with all her might at her "pa's" ire. John was to remain all night with Richard.

12--SOLOMON

Uncle Abram, also, was frequently treated with great brutality, although he was one of the kindest and most faithful creatures in the world. He was my cabin mate for years. There was a benevolent expression in the old man's face, pleasant to behold. He regarded us with a kind of parental feeling, always counseling us with remarkable gravity and deliberation.

Returning from Marshall's plantation one afternoon, whether I had been sent on some errand of the mistress, I found him lying on the cabin floor, his clothes saturated with blood. He informed me that he had been stabbed! While spreading cotton on the scaffold, haps came home intoxicated from Holmesville. He found fault with everything, giving many orders so directly contrary that it was impossible to execute any of them. Uncle Abraham, whose faculties were growing dull, became confused, and committed some blunder of no particular consequence. Epps was so enraged thereat, that, with drunken recklessness, he flew upon the old man, and stabbed him in the back.

It was a long, ugly wound, but did not happen to penetrate far enough to result fatally. It was sewed up by the mistress, who censored her husband with extreme severity, not only denouncing his inhumanity, but declaring that she expected nothing else than that he would bring the family to poverty--that he would kill all the slaves on the plantation in some of his drunken fits.

It was no uncommon thing with him to prostrate on Phebe with a chair or stick of wood; but the most cruel whipping that ever I was doomed to witness--one I can never recall with any other emotion than that of horror--was inflicted on the unfortunate Patsy.

It has been seen that the jealousy and hatred of mistress Epps made the daily life of her young and agile slave completely miserable. I am happy in the belief that on numerous occasions I was the means of averting punishment from the inoffensive girl. In Epps absence the mistress often ordered me to whip her without the remotest provocation. I would refuse, saying that I feared my masters displeasure, and several times ventured to remonstrate with her against the treatment Patsy received. I endeavored to impress her with the truth that the latter was not responsible for the acts of which she complained, but that she being a slave, and subject entirely to her masters will, he alone was answerable.

At length "the green eyed monster" crept into the soul of Epps also, and then it was that he joined with his wrathful wife in an infernal jubilee over the girl's miseries.

On a Sabbath day in hoeing time, not long ago, we were on the Bayou bank, washing our clothes, as was our usual custom. Presently Patsy was missing Epps called aloud, but there was no answer. 1 had observed her leaving the yard, and it was a wonder with us whether she had gone. In the course of a couple of hours she was seen approaching from the direction of Shaw's. This man, as has been intimated, was a notorious profligate, and withal not on the most friendly terms with Epps. Harriet, his black wife, knowing Patsy's troubles, was kinder to her, in consequence of which the latter was in the habit of going over to see her every opportunity. Her visits were prompted by friendship merely, but this suspicion gradually entered the brain of Epps, that another and a baser passion led her thither--that it was not Harriet she desired to meet, but rather the unblushing libertine, his neighbor. Patsy found her Master in a fearful rage on her return. His violence so alarmed her that at first she attempted to evade direct answers to his questions, which only served to increase his suspicions. She finally, however, drew herself up proudly, and in a spirit of indignation totally denied his charges.

"Missus don't give me soap to wash with, as she does the rest," said Patsy, "and you know why. I went over to Harriet's to get a piece," and saying this, she drew it forth from a pocket in her dress and exhibited it to him. "That's what I went to Shaw's for, Massa Epps," continued she; "the Lord knows that was all."

"You lie, you black wench!" shouted Epps.

"I don't lie, Massa. If you kill me, I'll stick to that."

"Oh! I'll fetch you down. I'll learn you to go to Shaw's. I'll take the stitch out of ye," he muttered fiercely through his shut teeth.

Then turning to me, he ordered four steaks to be driven into the ground, pointing with the toe of his boot to the places where he wanted them. When the stakes were driven down, he ordered her to be stripped of every article of dress. Ropes were then brought, and the naked girl was laid upon her face, her wrists and feet each tied firmly to a stake. Stepping to the Piazza, he took down a heavy whip, and placing it in my hands, commanded me to lash her. Unpleasant as it was, I was compelled to obey him. Nowhere that day, on the face of the whole earth, I ventured to say, was there such a demoniac exhibition witnessed as then ensued.

Mistress Epps stood on the Piazza among her children, gazing on the scene with an air of heartless satisfaction. The slaves were huddled together at a little distance, their countenances indicating the sorrow of their hearts. Poor Patsy prayed piteously for mercy, but her prayers were in vain. Epps ground his teeth, and stamped upon the ground, screaming at me, like a mad fiend, to strike harder.

"Or your turn will come next, you scoundrel," he yelled.

"Oh, mercy, massa!--oh! Have mercy, due. Oh, God! Pity me," Patsy exclaimed continually, struggling fruitlessly, and the flesh quivering at every stroke.

When I had struck her as many as 30 times, I stopped, and turned around towards Epps, hoping he was satisfied; But with bitter oaths and threats, he ordered me to continue. I inflicted 10 or 15 blows more. By the this time her back was covered with long welts, intersecting each other like network. Epps was yet furious and savage as ever, demanding if she would like to go to Shaw's again, and swearing he would flog her until she was she was in hell. Throwing down the whip, I declared I could punish her no more. He ordered me to go on, threatening me with a severe flogging than she had received, in case of refusal. My heart refolded at the inhuman scene, and risking the consequences, I absolutely refuse to raise the whip. He then ceased it himself, and applied with tenfold greater force than I had. The painful cries and shrieks of the tortured Patsy, mingling with a loud and angry curses of Epps, loaded the air. She was terribly lacerated-- I may say, without exaggeration, literally flayed. The lash was wet with blood, which flowed down her sides and dropped upon the ground. At length she seized A struggling. Her head sank listlessly on the ground. Her screams and supplications gradually decreased and died away into a low moan. She no longer writes and shrank beneath the lash when it bid out small pieces of her flesh. I thought that she was dying!

Patsy's life, especially after her whipping, was one long dream of liberty. Far away, to her fancy and immeasurable distance, she knew there was a land of freedom. 1000 times she had heard that somewhere in the distant North there were no slaves-- no masters. In her imagination it was an enchanted region, the paradise of the earth. To dwell where the black man may work for himself-- live in his own cabin-- till his own soil, was a blissful dream of Patsy's--a dream, alas! The fulfillment of which she could never realize.

The effect of these exhibitions of brutality on the household of the slaveholder, is apparent. Epps's oldest son is an intelligent lad of 10 or 12 years of age. It is pitiable, sometimes, to see him chastising, for instance, the venerable uncle Abram. He will call the old man to account, and if in his childish judgment it is necessary, sentence him to a certain number of lashes, which he proceeds to inflict with much gravity and deliberation. Mounted on his pony, he often rides into the field with his whip, playing the overseer, greatly to his father's delight. Without discrimination, at such times, he applies the rawhide, urging the slaves forward with shouts, and occasional expressions of profanity, while the old man laughs, and commends him as thorough-going boy.

"The child is the father to the man", and with such training, whatever may be his natural disposition, he could not well be otherwise than that, on arriving at maturity, the sufferings and miseries of the slave will be looked upon with entire indifference. The influence of the iniquitous system necessarily fosters an unfeeling and cruel spirit, Even in the bosoms of those who, among their equals, are regarded as humane and a generous.

Young Master Epps possessed some noble qualities, Yet no process of reasoning could lead him to comprehend, that in the eye of the almighty there is no distinction of color. He looked upon the black man simply as an animal, differing in no respect from any other animal, save in the gift of speech and the possession of somewhat higher instincts, and, therefore, the more valuable. To work Like his father's mules-- to be whipped and kicked and scourged through life--to address the white man with hat in hand, and eyes spent severely on the earth, in his mind, was the natural and proper destiny of the slave. Brought up with such ideas-- in the notion that we stand without the pale of humanity--no wonder the oppressors of my people are a pitiless and unrelenting race.

12-- ALBION

Among the peculiarities which marked the difference between Northern and Southern society was one so distinct and evident, one which had been so often illustrated in our political history, that it seems almost impossible that shrewd observers of that history should for a moment have overlooked or underestimated it. This is the influence of family position, social rank, or political prominence. Leadership, in the sense of a blind, unquestioning following of a man, without his being the peculiar exponent of an idea, is a thing almost unknown at the North : at the South it is a power. Every family there has its clientage, its followers, who rally to its lead as quickly, and with almost as unreasoning a faith, as the old Scottish clansmen, summoned by the burning cross. By means of this fact slavery had been perpetuated for fifty years. It was through this peculiarity that secession and rebellion became dominant there. This fact seems to have been dimly recognized, though not at all understood or appreciated, by those who originated what are known as the Reconstruction Acts. They seem to have supposed, that, if this class were deprived of actual political position, they would thereby be shorn of political influence : so it was provided that all who had any such prominence as to have been civil or military officers before the war, and had afterwords engaged in rebellion, should not be allowed to vote, or hold office, until relieved from such disability.

It was a fatal mistake. The dead leader has always more followers than his living peer. Every henchman of those lordlings at whom this blow was aimed felt it far more keenly than he would if it had lighted on his own cheek. The king of every village was dethroned ; the magnate of every crossroads was degraded. Henceforward, each and every one of their satellites was bound to eternal hostility toward these measures and to all that might result therefrom.

So the line of demarcation was drawn. Upon the one side were found only those who constituted what was termed respectable people, — the bulk of those of the white race who had ruled the South in ante antebellum days, who had fostered slavery, and been fattened by it, who had made it the dominant power in the nation, together with the mass of those whose courage and capacity had organized rebellion, and led the South in that marvelous struggle for separation. On the other side were the pariahs of the land, to designate the different classes of which, three words were used : "Niggers," the newly-enfranchised African voters ; " Scalawags," the native whites who were willing to accept the reconstruction measures ; and " Carpetbaggers," all men of Northern birth, resident in the South, who should elect to speak or act in favor of such reconstruction.

The ban of proscription spared neither age nor sex, and was never relaxed. In business or pleasure, in friendship or religion, in the market or the church, it was omnipresent. Men were excluded from the Lord's Communion for establishing sabbath schools for colored people. Those who did not curse the measure, its authors, and the government by which it was administered, were henceforth shunned as moral and social lepers. The spirit of the dead Confederacy was stronger than the mandate of the nation to which it had succumbed in battle.

Editor: Servosse later spoke at a political meeting. There were what might be known as 'closet' Union men, who privately supported Servosse, but dared not say so publicly. After the meeting, Servosse has a private conversation with one of the attendees.

" That is what we want. I tell you it did me good to hear you : but you must look out ! You don't know these people as I do. It don't do to speak out here as you do at the North."

But why not? " he would query impatiently. " That was my honest conviction : why should I not speak it out ? "

Hush. hush ! " his interviewer would say nervously. "Here, let's step aside a little while, and chat."

And then, perhaps, they would pass out of the public way, into that refuge of free thought at the South, the woods (or the bushes," as the scraggly growth is more generally termed); and he would listen to some tale of heroic endurance by which his companion had evaded conscription in the time of the war, or avoided prosecution in the ante-war era, which elicited his wonder both for the devotion then displayed for principle, and the caution which was born of it.

" Why do you not speak out ?" he would ask.

" Oh, it won't do ! I could not live here, or not in any peace at least, if I did ; and then my family — they would be cut off from all society : nobody would have any thing to do with them. Why, as careful as I have been, my children are insulted every now and then as 'nigger-worshipers,' and — and" —

" And what ? "

" Well--Yankee-lovers,' " apologetically. " You see, it's got out in my neighborhood that I came to see you a few weeks ego."

"Well, what of that ? Haven't you a right to do so ? Can't s man speak his opinions, and act his preferences ? "

" You will find out that this old pro-slavery, aristocratic element don't allow people to differ from them peaceably and quietly. If I were you, I'd be mighty careful who I talked to. You don't know any thing about what trouble you may get into any day."

" Well, I shall not," the Fool would reply. " I don't care any thing particular about the matter. I am no politician, and don't want to be ; but I am going to say just what I think, at all proper times and places, when the spirit moves me so to do."

" Of course, of course," would be the reply. " You know best ; but you ought to recollect that you are not at the North, where they allow every man to have his own opinions, and rather despise him if he don't have them, as I take it they do."

So the two men would separate, each wondering at the other ; the Fool amazed that one could endure so much for the sake of his own opinion, think so well, apprehend so clearly the state of affairs, and yet be so timid about declaring his convictions. He could not call it cowardice ; for many of these men had taken their lives in their hands to shelter men on their way to the Union lines. Others, in the ante-war era, had circulated books and pamphlets in regard to slavery, to be found in possession of which was a capital crime. Others had helped fugitive slaves to escape to freedom, with the terrors of Judge Lynch's rope and fagots before their eyes. Others still, upon being conscripted into the Confederate ranks, had refused to bear arms, even when put into the front rank and under the hottest fire of battle.

They could look at danger and death very calmly ; but they could not stand forth openly, and face the glare of social proscription. The Fool could not understand it.

On the other hand, the Southern Unionists could not understand the heedless outspokenness of the Northern man. To them it seemed the very height of folly. It meant proscription, broils, mobs, and innumerable risks which might be avoided by a prudent silence.

13

13-- CORNELIA

In the course of a few years prospects began to brighten for the planters, as far as getting up their places was concerned ; but the negroes, getting accustomed to their freedom and influenced by the demoralizing politics of the day, became lazier each year and imposed on their former masters, refusing to work if they did not feel in the humor, though they lived in the owner's cottages and raised their stock and fowl at his expense, finding it easy to subsist (which was the only ambition of most of them) with a cottage, garden, stock, and fowls in a balmy climate.

They lounged around luxuriously, hanging over fences as is their way to this day, strolled leisurely over the green fields, wandered aimlessly through the woods, picked the banjo, and thought life at last worth living. The planters were not in circumstances to afford such trifling, and did not value their own lives very highly if such proceedings continued to be the order of the day, and searching far and near for more ambitious tillers of the soil, finally availed themselves of some Chinese coolies who seemed to be giving satisfaction in the West Indies and California.

To give them a trial, at any rate, would be no less disastrous than the present situation, and in due time a large number were installed on many of the plantations at very high wages, always in gold, and one of the number was paid to do the cooking. These worked in gangs of from twenty to forty, or even fifty ; wore Chinese costumes, carried tea to the fields, and drank it all day instead of water. They always had a kite flying, and took it to the fields with them. This kite had a bow on it. When the kite darted around the bow-string, made a noise, then the Chinese all looked up and said something.

At night the kite was tied to the gable of the house. Inside they had a little joss with a taper burning before him at all hours, and when any one of them died they covered the grave, or mound, with cooked food. The house they occupied at the White Castle stood in the pasture, and the hogs had gotten under it, infesting it with fleas.

A Chinaman went to the overseer and told him there was " too muchee buggee " in that house. When the overseer finally understood what was meant, he asked him why he did not catch them. The Chinaman replied: " Too muchee jumpee." The Chinamen did not answer the purpose. If they found the crop in grass, or grinding season coming on, they did not regard their contracts, but struck for higher wages. They thought so much of their comfort they used fans continually. Even when they were plowing they had them stuck up their backs, under the shirt, where they could conveniently reach them. About twenty of them would crowd in three rooms, making their bunks over each other against the wall, with a piece of matting put down for a mattress, and two blocks joined by a plank for a pillow. They ate with chop-sticks out of a bowl and used benches either side of a long table—instead of chairs—squatting upon them. They ate rice principally, and anything else they could find. Some turkeys died of cholera. Upon their request for them being granted, the Chinese cooked and served them for a meal. Excuse the feeling this gives rise to, but it is true.

13-- SOLOMON

In the month of June,1852, in pursuance of a previous contract, Mr. Avery, a Carpenter of Bayou Rouge, commenced the erection of a house for Master Epps. It has previously been stated that there are no cellars on Bayou Boeuf; on the other hand, such is the low and swampy nature of the ground, the great houses are usually built upon spiles. Another peculiarity is, the rooms are not plastered, but the ceiling and the sides are covered with matched Cypress boards, painted such color as most pleases the owner's taste. Generally the plank and boards are sawed by slaves with whipsaws, there being no water power upon which mills might be built within many miles. When the planter erects for himself a dwelling, therefore, there is plenty of extra work for his slaves. Having had some experience under Tibeats as a carpenter, I was taken from the field altogether, on the arrival of Avery and his hands.

Among them was one to whom I owe an immeasurable depth of gratitude. Only for him, in all probability, I should have ended my days in slavery. He was my deliverer--a man whose true heart over-flowed with noble and generous emotions. To the last moment of my existence I shall remember him with feelings of thankfulness. His name was Bass, and at that time he resided in Marksville. It will be difficult to convey a correct impression of his appearance or character. He was a large man, between 40 and 50 years old, of light complexion and light hair. He was very cool and self possessed, fond of argument, but always speaking with extreme deliberation. He was that kind of person whose peculiarity of manner was such that nothing he uttered ever gave offence. What would be intolerable, coming from the lips of another, could be said by him with impunity. There was not a man on Red River, perhaps, that agreed with him on the subject of politics or religion, and not a man, I venture to say, who discussed either of those subjects half as much. It seemed to be taken for granted that he would espouse the unpopular side of every local question, and it always cre-ated amusement rather than displeasure among his auditors, to lis-ten to the ingenious and original manner in which he maintained the controversy. He was a bachelor—an "old bachelor," according to the true acceptation of the term--having no kindred living, as he knew of, in the world. Neither had he any permanent abiding place--wander-ing from one state to another, as his fancy dictated. He had lived in Marksville three or four years, and in the prosecution of his business as a Carpenter; and in consequence, likewise, of his peculiarities, was quite extensively known throughout the parish of Avoyelles. He was

liberal to a fault; and his many acts of kindness and transparent goodness of heart rendered him popular in the community, the sentiment
of which he unceasingly combated.

He was a native of Canada, from whence he had wandered in early
life, and after visiting all the principal localities in the northern and
western states, in the course of his peregrinations, arrived in the un-
healthy region of the Red River. His last removal was from Illinois.
Whether he has now gone, I regret to be obliged to say, is unknown to
me. He gathered up his effects and departed quietly from Marksville
the day before I did, the suspicions of his instrumentality in procuring
my liberation rendering such high step necessary. For the Commission of a just and righteous act he would undoubtedly have suffered
a death, had he remained within reach of the slave whipping tribe on
Bayou Boeuf.

One day, while working on the House, Bass and Epps became engaged in a controversy, to which, as will be readily supposed, I listened
with absorbing interest. They were discussing the subject of slavery.

"I tell you what it is Epps," said Bass, "it's all wrong-- all wrong,
Sir--there is no justice nor righteousness in it. I wouldn't own a slave
if I was rich as Croesus, which I am not, as is perfectly well understood, more particularly among my creditors. There's another hum-
bug-- the credit system-- humbug, sir; no credit-- no debt. Credit
leads Amen into temptation. Cash down is the only thing that will de-
liver him from evil. But this question of slavery; What right have you
to your when you come down to the point?"

"What right!" said Epps, laughing; "why, I bought 'em and paid for
'em."

"Of course you did; the law says you have the right to hold a nigger,
but begging the law's pardon, it lies. Yes, Epps, when the law says that,
it's a liar, and the truth is not in it. Is everything right because the law
allows it? Suppose they pass a law taking away your liberty and making you a slave?"

"Oh, that ain't a supposable case," said Epps, still laughing; "hope you don't compare me to a nigger, Bass."

"Well," Bass answered gravely, "no, not exactly. But I have seen niggers before now as good as I am, and I have no acquaintance with any white man in these parts that I consider a whit better than myself. Now, in the sight of God, what is the difference, Epps, between a white man and a black one?"

"All the difference in the world," replied Epps." You might as well ask what the difference is between a white man and a baboon. Now, I've seen one of those critters in Orleans that knowed just as much as any nigger I've got. You'd call them feller citizens, I 'spose?"--and Epps indulged in a loud laugh at his own wit.

"Look here, Epps," continued his companion; "you can't laugh me down in that way. Some men are witty, and some aren't so witty as they think they are. Now let me ask you a question. Are all men created free and equal as the Declaration of Independence holds they are?"

"Yes," responded Epps, "but all men; niggers, and monkeys ain't;" And here upon he broke forth into a more boisterous laugh than before.

"There are monkeys among white people as well as black, when you come down to that," coolly remarked Bass. "I know some white men that use arguments no sensible monkey would. But let that pass. These niggers are human beings. If they don't know as much as their masters, whose fault is it? They are not allowed to know anything. You have books and papers, and can go where you please, and gather intelligence in 1000 ways. But your slaves have no privileges. You'd whip one of them if caught reading a book. They are held in bondage generation after generation, deprived of mental improvement, and who can expect them to possess much knowledge? If they are brought down to a level with the brute of creation, you slaveholders will never be blamed for it. If they are baboons, or stand no higher in the scale of intelligence than such animals, you and men like you will have to answer for it. There's a sin, a fearful sin, resting on this nation, that will not go unpunished forever. There will be a reckoning yet-- yes, Epps, there's a day coming that will burn you as an oven. It may be sooner or it may be later, but it's a coming as sure as the Lord is just."

"If you lived up among the Yankees in New England," said Epps, "I expect you'd be one of them cursed fanatics that know more than the constitution, and go about peddling clocks and coaxing niggers to run away".

"If I was in New England," returned Bass, "I would be just what I am here. I would say that slavery was an iniquity, and ought to be abolished. I would say there was no reason nor justice in the law, or the constitution that allows one man to hold another in bondage. It wouldn't be hard for you to lose your property, to be sure, but it wouldn't be half as hard as it would be to lose your liberty. You have no more right to your freedom, in exact justice, then Uncle Abram yonder. Talk about the black skin, and black blood; Why, how many slaves are there on this Bayou is white is either of us? And what difference is there in the color of the soul? Pshaw! The whole system is as absurd as it is cruel. You may own niggers and a be hanged, but I wouldn't own one for the best plantation in Louisiana."

"You like to hear yourself talk, Bass, better than any man I know of. You would argue that black was white, or white black, if anybody would contradict you. Nothing suits you in this world, and I don't believe you will be satisfied with the next, if you should have your choice in them."

Conversations substantially like the foregoing were not unusual between the two after this; Epps drawing him out more for the purpose of creating a laugh at his expense, then with a view of fairly discussing the merits of the question. He looked upon Bass, as a man ready to say anything merely for the pleasure of hearing his own voice; as somewhat self conceited, perhaps, contending against his faith and judgment, in order, simply, to exhibit his dexterity in argumentation.

He remained at Epps' through the summer, visiting Marksville generally once a fortnight. The more I saw of him, the more I became convinced he was a man in whom I could confide. Nevertheless, my previous ill fortune had taught me to be extremely cautious. It was not my place to speak to a white man except when spoken to, but I omitted no opportunity of throwing myself in his way, and endeavored constantly in every possible manner to attract his attention. In the early part of August he and myself were at work alone in the house, the other carpenters having left, and Epps being absent in the field. Now was the time, if ever, to broach the subject, and I resolved to do it, and submit to whatever consequences might ensue. We were busily at work in the afternoon, when I stopped suddenly and said—

"Master Bass, I want to ask you what part of the country you came from?"

"Why, Platt, what put that into your head?" He answered. "You wouldn't know if I should tell you." After a moment or two he added—" I was born in Canada; now guess where that is."

"Oh, I know where Canada is, I have been there myself."

"Yes, I expect you are well acquainted all through that country," he remarked, laughing incredulously.

"Yeah sure as I live, Master Bass," I replied," I have been there. I have been in Montreal and Kingston, in Queenston, and a great many places in Canada, and I have been in York State, too--in Buffalo, and Rochester, and Albany, and can tell you the names of the villages on the Erie Canal and the Champlain canal."

Bass turned round and gazed at me a long time without uttering a syllable.

"How came you here?" he inquired, at length.

"Master Bass," I answered, "if justice had been done, I never would have been here."

"Well, how's this?" Said he. "Who are you? You have been in Canada sure enough; I know all the places you mentioned. How did you happen to get here? Come, tell me all about it."

"I have no friends here," was my reply," that I can put confidence in. I am afraid to tell you, though I don't believe you would tell Master Epps if I should."

He assured me earnestly he would keep every word I might speak to him a profound secret, and in his curiosity was evidently strongly excited. It was a long story, I informed him, and would take some time to relate it. Master Epps would be back soon, but if he would see me that night after all were asleep, I would repeat it to him. He consented readily to the arrangement, and directed me to come into the building where we were then at work, and I would find him there. About midnight, when all was still and quiet, I crept cautiously from my cabin, and silently entering the unfinished building, found him awaiting me.

After further assurances on his part that I should not be betrayed, I began a relation of the history of my life and misfortunes. He was deeply interested, asking numerous questions in reference to localities and events. Having ended my story I besought him to write to some of my friends at the north, acquainting them with my situation, and begging them to forward free papers, and take such steps as they might consider proper to secure my release. He promised to do so, but dwelt upon the danger of such an act in case of detection, and now impressed upon me the great necessity of strict silence and secrecy. Before we parted our plan of operation was arranged.

We agreed to meet the next night at a specified place among the high weeds on the bank of the bayou, some distance from the master's dwelling. There he was to write down on paper the names and addresses of several persons, old friends in the North, to whom he would direct letters during his next visit to Marksville. It was not deemed prudent to meet in the new house, inasmuch as the light it would be necessary to use might possibly be discovered. In the course of the day I managed to obtain a few matches and a piece of candle, unperceived, from the kitchen, during a temporary absence of Aunt Phebe. Bass had pencil and paper in his tool chest.

At the appointed hour we met on the Bayou bank, and creeping among the high weeds, I lighted the candle, while he drew forth pencil and paper and prepared for business. I gave him the names of William Perry, Cephas Parker and Judge Marvin, all of Saratoga Springs, Saratoga County, New York. I had been employed by the latter in the United States Hotel, and had a transacted business with the former to a considerable extent, and trusted that at least one of them would be still living at that place. He carefully wrote the names, and then remarked, thoughtfully--

"It is so many years since you left Saratoga, all these men may be dead, or may be removed. You say you obtained papers at the custom house in New York. Probably there is a record of them there, and I think it would be well too right and ascertain."

I agreed with him, and again repeated the circumstances related heretofore, connected with my visit to the custom house with Brown and Hamilton. We lingered on the Bank of the Bayou and hour or more, conversing upon the subject which now engrossed our thoughts. I could no longer doubt his fidelity, and freely spoke to him of the many sorrows I had borne in silence, and so long. I spoke of my wife and children, mentioning their names and ages, and dwelling upon the unspeakable happiness it would be to clasp them to my heart once more before I died. I caught him by the hand, and with tears and passionate entreaties implored him to befriend me--to restore me to my kindred and to liberty--promising I would weary heaven the remainder of my life with prayers that it would bless and prosper him. In the enjoyment of freedom--surrounded by the associations of youth, and restored to the bosom of my family--that promise is not yet forgotten, nor shall it ever be so long as I have strength to raise my imploring eyes on high.

"Oh, blessings on his kindly voice and on his silver hair, and blessings on his whole life long, until he meet me there."

He overwhelmed me with assurances of friendship and faithfulness, saying he had never before taken so deep an interest in the fate of anyone. He spoke of himself in a somewhat mournful tone, as a lonely man, a wanderer about the world--that he was growing old, and must soon reach the end of his earthly journey, and lie down to his final rest without kith or kin to mourn for him, or to remember him--that his life was of little value to himself, and henceforth should be devoted to the accomplishment of my liberty, and to an unceasing warfare against the accursed shame of slavery.

After this time we seldom spoke to, or recognized each other. He was, moreover, less free in his conversation with Epps on the subject of slavery. The remotest suspicion that there was any unusual intimacy--any secret understanding between us--never once entered the mind of Epps, or any other person, white or black, on the plantation.

I am often asked, with an air of incredulity, how i succeeded so many years in keeping from my daily and constant companions the knowledge of my true name and history. The terrible lesson Burch taught me, impressed indelibly upon my mind the danger and uselessness of asserting I was a freeman. There was no possibility of any slave being able to assist me, while, on the other hand, there was a possibility of his exposing me. When it is recollected the whole current of my thoughts, for 12 years, turned to the contemplation of escape, it will not be wondered at, that I was always cautious and on my guard. It would have been an act of folly to have proclaimed my right to freedom; it would only have subjected me to severe scrutiny--probably have consigned me to some more distant and inaccessible region than even Bayou Boeuf. Edwin Epps was a person utterly regardless of a black man's rights or wrongs--utterly destitute of any natural sense of justice, as I well know. It was important, therefore, not only as regarded my hope of deliverance, but also as regarded the few personal privileges I was permitted to enjoy, to keep him from the history of my life.

The Saturday night subsequent to our interview at the water's edge, Bass went home to Marksville. The next day, being Sunday, employed himself in his own room writing letters. One he directed to the collector of customs at New York, another to Judge Marvin, and another to Messrs. Parker and Perry jointly. The latter was the one which led to my recovery. He subscribed my true name, but in the postscript intimated I was not the writer. The letter itself shows that he considered himself engaged in a dangerous undertaking--no less than running "the risk of his life, if detected."

The allusion to myself in the work recently issued, entitled "A Key to Uncle Tom's Cabin," contains the first part of this letter, omitting the postscript. Neither are the full names of the gentleman to whom it is directed correctly stated, there being a slight discrepancy, probably a typographical error. To the postscript more than to the body of the communication am I indebted for my liberation, as will presently be seen.

When Bass returned from Marksville he informed me of what he had done. We continued our midnight consultations, never speaking to each other through the day, accepting as it was necessary about the work. As nearly as he was able to ascertain, it would require two weeks for the letter to reach Saratoga in due course of mail, hand at the same length of time for an answer to return. Within six weeks, had the farthest, we concluded, and answer would arrive, if it arrived at all. A great many suggestions were now made, and a great deal of conversation took place between us, as to the most safe and proper course to pursue on receipt of the free papers. They would stand between him and harm, in case we were overtaken and arrested leaving the country altogether. It would be known infringement of law, however much it might provoke individual hostility, to assist a freeman to regain his freedom.

At the end of four weeks he was again at Marksville, but no answer had arrived. I was sorely disappointed, but still reconciled myself with the reflection that's sufficient a length of time had not yet elapsed that there might have been delays-- and that I could not reasonably expect one so soon. 6, 7, 8, and ten weeks passed by, however, and nothing came. I was in a fever of suspense whenever Bass visited Marksville, and could scarcely close my eyes until his return. Finally my master's house was finished, and the time came when Bass must leave me. The night before his departure I was wholly given up to despair. I had clung to him as a drowning man clings to the floating spar, knowing if it slips from his grasp he must forever sink beneath the waves. The all glorious hope, upon which I had delayed such eager hold, was crumbling into ashes in my hands. I felt as if sinking down, down, I amidst the bitter waters of slavery, from the unfathomable depths of which I should never rise again.

The generous heart of my friend and benefactor was touched with pity at the sight of my distress. He endeavored to cheer me up, promising to return the day before Christmas, and if no intelligence was received in the meantime, some further step would be undertaken to effect our design. He exhorted me to keep up my spirits-- to rely upon his continued efforts in my behalf, assuring me, in most earnest and impressive language, that my liberation should, from thenceforth, be the chief object of his thoughts.

In his absence the time passed slowly indeed. I looked forward to Christmas with intense anxiety and impatience. I had about given up the expectation of receiving any answer to the letters they might have miscarried, or might have been misdirected. Perhaps those at Saratoga, to whom they had been addressed, were all dead; perhaps, engaged in their pursuits, they did not consider the fate of an obscure, unhappy black man of sufficient importance to be noticed. My whole reliance was in Bass. The faith I had in him was continually reassuring me, and enabled me to stand up against the tide of disappointment that had overwhelmed me. So wholly was I Absorbed in reflecting upon my situation and prospects, that the hands with whom I labored in the field often observed it. Patsy would ask me if I was sick, and Uncle Abram, and Bob, and Wiley frequently expressed a curiosity to know what I could be thinking about so steadily. But I evaded their inquiries with some light remark, and kept my thoughts locked closely in my breast.

13—ALBION

Editor: After the civil war, as part of Reconstruction, the various confederate states held constitutional conventions to reestablish laws in these former confederate states, within the dictates of the 13th 14th and 15th amendments recently passed by the US Congress. Albion Tourgee would become a delegate to the North Carolina constitutional convention. Here is an abbreviated description of the meeting to determine a delegate from their district.

When the time for the election of delegates to a constitutional convention was near at hand, the union men of the county held a meeting to nominate candidates. The colored people, as yet unused to political assemblages, but with an indistinct impression that their rights and interests were involved, attended in large numbers, the union men were few, and not of that class who were accustomed to the lead and control of such meetings. The place of assembly selected was an old count country schoolhouse some 2 miles from the county seat and situated in a beautiful Grove the colored people had gathered in a dense mass on one side of the of the platform, waiting in earnest expectancy to take whatever part might be allotted to them in the performance of the new and untried duties of citizenship. The white men were squatted about in little groups, conversing in low, uneasy tones, and glancing suspiciously at every newcomer. A little at one side was Colonel Ezekiel Vaughan, with a few cronies, laughing and talking boisterously about the different men who were taking part in the movement.

" Why don't you open your show, Servosse ?" asked Vaughn, in a loud and taunting voice, as he approached the group. "I tell you we are getting mighty tired of waiting; and them niggers is just bustin' for a chance to begin votin'."

" Hello, Vaughn!" said the Fool, in a voice equally loud, but more jovial. "Are you here ? Then we will begin at once. We were just waiting for the monkey before the show began; but, if you are on hand, we are all ready."

There was a laugh, and Vaughn retired disconcerted. But one of those with whom the Fool had been conversing drew him aside, and said with great seriousness, —

"Now, Colonel, you will excuse me ; but I am afraid you will get yourself into trouble if you talk to these folks in that way. You see they are not used to it."

"Then let them get used to it," said the Fool carelessly. "If Vaughn did not want a sharp retort, he should not have made an insolent remark."

"That's so, Colonel; but you see they are used to doin' and sayin' any thing they choose in regard to people who happen to differ with them. Why, I remember when a man was prosecuted here in this very county for havin' a seditious book — one about slavery, you know — in his possession, and lendin' it to a friend ; and people were almost afraid to speak to him, or go bail for him. You Northern people don't know any thing about what we call public opinion here."

"I'm sure I don't want to know, if it means that a man shall not speak his opinion freely, and throw stones when another throws them at him," said the Fool determinedly.

" Yet," said the Union man, "it is folly to defy and provoke such a spirit unnecessarily."

"I agree with you there, my friend," was the Fool's answer. "But, if one has principles which are worth supporting or fighting for, they ought also to be worth standing up for against ridicule and arrogance."

"It would seem so ; but it won't do, — not in this country, anyhow," said the Unionist with a sigh.

At this point there were symptoms of excitement among the crowd; and a faint, straggling cheer broke out, as Colonel Rhenn rode up, and dismounted from his horse, which he tied to an overhanging bough, and came forward, holding his well-worn beaver hat in his left hand, bowing, and shaking hands with his neighbors, and returning with slight but grave courtesy the boisterous greeting of the colored people. This arrival at once seemed to give confidence to those who had before evidently regarded the movement as a disagreeable if not a dangerous duty. Nathan Rhenn was a gentleman of a type peculiarly Southern, and exceedingly rare. He was of an old but not now wealthy family. His connections were good, but not high. Before the war he had been in comfortable circumstances only : now he was actually poor. Yet at no time had he abated one jot of that innate gentility which had always marked his deportment. He was clad now in " butternut-gray " homespun, wore black woolen gloves on his hands, a high black stock on his neck, with a high, narrow-brimmed, and rather dingy beaver hat, and would have been a figure highly provocative of mirth, had it not been for his considerate, graceful, and self-respecting courtesy. Since the meeting at which he presided, when the Fool made his maiden speech upon a political question, Colonel Rhenn had rarely attended public meetings, and was known as one whose status (despite his former Unionism, which was unquestioned) was very doubtful. He was known to be one who would not have attended the meeting unless he intended to give in his adhesion to the cause which it had assembled to promote. He was considered, therefore, an accession of very great importance, by those who were present, to the cause of Reconstruction. Hardly had he greeted his many friends, when some one arose and said, —

" I nominate Nathan Rhenn as chairman of this meeting."

It was unanimously concurred in; And the new arrival, with many grave bows and protestations, permitted himself to be led to the platform. Upon taking his seat as chairman, he made a brief speech, in substance as follows:

FELLOW-CITIZENS, —I have come here to-day for the purpose of giving my support and countenance to a movement in support of what are known as the Reconstruction Acts, which I presume to be the reason that you have honored me by making me your chairman. As you are well aware, I have always been a Union man. I believe that under all circumstances, and by all persons and parties, I have been accorded that distinction. At the same time, I have never been, or been considered, an abolitionist. I was a slaveholder, and belonged to a race of slaveholders, and never felt any conscientious scruples at remaining such. I did not pass upon slavery, it is true, as a new or an abstract question, but considered it as I found it, solely in relation to myself. I did not buy nor sell, except when I bought a woman that she might not be sold away from her husband, and sold one man, at his own request, that he might go with his wife. The act of buying and selling human beings, I admit, was repulsive to me; but I accepted the institution as I found it, and did not feel called upon to attempt its overthrow. In the attempt which was made to disrupt the government, this institution has been destroyed; and it is the question in regard to the future political relations of those who were, as it were, but yesterday slaves, which produces the present differences of opinion among our people, and promises future conflict. If it were the simple question whether we should now be restored to the American Union, and take our place as one of the co-ordinate States, which we had to decide, there would be no difference of opinion. Only an insignificant minority of our people would oppose such restoration upon any terms which did not embrace the conferring of political power upon the freed people. Many think this an unwise and impracticable measure : others believe it to be imposed upon us by the conquerors, simply as an act of wanton and gross insult, for the purpose of adding to the degradation of an already humiliated foe. The fact, also, that every one who had been an officer of the old government, and then served the Confederacy in any voluntary capacity, is barred from the right of suffrage, while his recent slave is given the power to vote, occasions much ill feeling. While I deem the exclusion wise and necessary, though it must strike some who are undeserving, I confess that I have had my fears in regard to the latter measure. After mature and earnest reflection, however, I have become satisfied, that, at the least, the best thing we can do is to accept what is offered, show our willingness to submit to whatever may be deemed wise and proper, and trust that the future may establish the right. Therefore I have come here today to co-operate with you. And now, gentlemen, what is your pleasure?"

For once there was a scarcity of candidates. No one seemed to desire a position which promised to be onerous, without honor, and of little profit; which it was felt would cast odium

Editor--Servosse (Tourgee) would be selected as the delegate based on the following platform.

1. Equal civil and political rights to all men.
2. The abolition of property qualifications for voters, officers, and jurors.
3. Election by the people of all officers have been- legislative, executive, and judicial-- in the state, the counties, the municipalities.
4. Penal Reform the abolition of the whipping post, the stocks, and the branding iron; and the reduction of capital felonies from 17 to one, or at most 2
5. Uniform and ad valorem taxation upon property, and a limitation of capitation tax to not more than three days labor upon the public roads in each year, Or an equivalent thereof.
6. An effective system of public schools.

14

14--CORNELIA

" Will you go down to dinner with me ? " said a bright-eyed, rosy-cheeked damsel at my elbow, as I was standing among a crowd of girls at the head of the stairs leading to the refectory of a large, select boarding school in the North, that our Southernized Yankee rector, whom we all loved at home, had recommended to my parents, and who though a red-hot Southerner after dwelling in the South for several years, still remembered some good things he had seen in the North. The girl mentioned above was a Northern girl, and her name was Helen Hancock. I had been here but a few hours ; not long enough to make any selection of friends, but she being one that would attract attention in a crowd, I accepted the proffered arm, which was soon put around my waist, I following suit ; so here we were, a little Confederate and a little Yankee embracing one another, only a few years after the war. In this manner one of my lifelong friends was made. Later she introduced me to her cousin, Ethel Banks, and we formed a trio of friendship. It is so much easier to make a friend than to give one up, should one discover her afterward undesirable, that I took my mother's advice in parting, and was rather chary of falling right in with strangers at once, but I have ever been glad that I followed here my animal instincts, which, according to Mr. Darwin, we all possess (?) to a certain degree.

After grace had been said and we were all seated at the tables, I took the opportunity to observe my surroundings, as I had not yet caught the drift of the favorite topics of the girls present and was not much interested in their chatter, though I did not mind in the least seeing things lively, for I had heard that at some schools the girls were not permitted to speak at table, and I did not doubt that I would do my full share later on.

There were three immense tables, arranged in the shape of a horse-shoe, at which far more than a hundred girls were seated every day.

I did not know whether to feel honored or not, according to my way of thinking, when the girls told me that Queen Emma, of the Sandwich Islands, had been educated here, but imagined from the gusto with which it was told that I ought to feel so. In due time they also made me aware of the fact that it was the first girls' school which England had recognized as a school in the United States, and tried to emphasize it by getting one of the teachers to show me some pieces of silver for the church we attended in the village, which had been presented by Her Royal Highness, Queen Anne, she having taken an interest in the church, with which the school seemed connected.

Whether either of the Queens had anything to do with it or not, I was very happy there. Possibly their good angels inspired me with a wholesome feeling, for we read of the worthiness of both.

There were hard lessons to be learned and a difficult course to be pursued, rules to be obeyed for the easy working of the school system, and I can truly say I never saw such a well-regulated household, nor can I imagine a better. The teachers commanded our respect by their learning and refinement, and the girls, catching their courtesy,were companionable and obliging. I never felt more at home anywhere.

About every six weeks a concert was given, and soon after my arrival I was called upon to play on the piano as a test of my ability and progress, rather more than for the pleasure they knew I might impart, I imagined, but I awoke next morning to find myself quite famous among the girls as far as their appreciation of my music was concerned, and after receiving some nice compliments from the teachers I was translated to the parlor for my music lessons, which was the acme, and the professor was to instruct me. Not until then did I realize what my German professor at home had meant when he called me a " fine performer." And as the years roll on I appreciate it more and more, for it was so much more genuine than the hollow praises of the outer world, that are more often prompted by selfish motives than from a true knowledge of the subject.

Many and many a time did a friend break the rules and slip in my music-room during practicing hours to hear what she said she thought was the sweetest voice in the world—though I did not pride myself on that—and in my innocent vanity, reader, I sometimes wished I could—for awhile—be some one else for the purpose of listening to myself, I loved music so. In after life, when my heart at times was sore with the ways of the world, and hope forbade me be sure there was a better, it was a comfort and solace, also a spur, to look upward, to revert to the life I had led at this institution, based entirely upon the footsteps of " The Master," each rewarded first for her goodness or pretty conduct, next for her intellect, drawing out all that was noblest and best in each individual. And I honor the strong men and women who took the lead in this good work ; forming women who developed a fine principle, a self-poise and an equanimity which dreads no future, shirks no duty, but ever looks with trusting heart for the glories which await them beyond and the " well done, thou good and faithful servant," which after the pomps and vanities of the world have been tasted seems the true pleasure.

Of course, the Northern girls wanted to know all about blood-hounds and ku-kluxes, and really viewed me with wide-open eyes when I asseverated that I had never seen any, and I really believe I lost a part of my prestige from my assertion of the fact. They wanted to know if our houses were plastered, if we had oysters and ice in the South. I wondered if I looked such a Hottentot, to elicit such surmises.

Flags were flying, and the usual demonstrations of the Fourth of July were in progress. As the South had not taken much interest in it since the war, I was not enthusiastic, but simply looked forward to a holiday which had some pleasant functions in view —nice walks and talks, free from the usual restrictions of school life, on what we called " The Circle," a large plot of ground at the back of the building, with a lengthy walk sweeping around. After breakfast and the usual morning services, we went over in a body to the Bishop's residence., A few doors from hours, by invitation. This was always one of the features of the 4th, and a pleasant one.

The Bishop's wife was aimable to a degree, and would have taken me there, no doubt, but I hesitated to have any seeming partiality shown me. After dinner we went out under the trees. Helen Hancock and Ethel Banks, my chums, and myself were arm in arm, walking along, discussing the different affairs of the day, when I noticed the United States flag floating over our path, but we had not yet reached it. Stopping suddenly, I told them I was not going under that flag. I always wanted to be courteous. And up to this time I had said or done nothing which could be noticed to dash cold water on the day, They both seemed surprised and said that they did not know I had any such foolish prejudices. I said, it was no prejudiced but a principle with me and that I would walk around it and meet them on the other side, proceeding to do so. Some other girls coming along, My decision was communicated to them, as I walked slowly myself around, outside of the flag, for I was interested to know what the outcome would be, and listen the while.

By the time I reached the other side, my weakness, if they chose to call it such-- though it required much strength of purpose-- was known all over the grounds, I could tell by the commotion. As Helen and Ethel now hastened up to join me, a shout of applause from a sprinkling of Southern girls, who had been indifferent or devoid of daring before, greeted me, And the Northern girls said I was right plucky, and that they did not mind, Though some of them tried to pull me under the flag for fun, and other slightly endeavoured to make me forget and walk under, But I was weary, and never did. Still I wondered what the teachers might think when it got to their ears, as most everything did. One of them was kind enough to say if I adhere to every principle in future, as firmly as I had to this, she had no fears for me. She being the leader, I was much relieved, as I did not wish to hurt anyone's feelings.

14 -SOLOMON

When he was gone I obtained a pass, and started for Tanner's--not Peter Tanner's, Of whom mention has previously been made, but a relative of his. I played during the day and most of the night, spending the next day, Sunday, in my cabin. Monday I crossed the Bayou to Douglas Marshall's, all Epps slaves accompanying me, and on Tuesday went to the old Norwood place, which is the third plantation above Marshall's, on the same side of the water.

This is estate is now owned by miss Mary McCoy, a lovely girl, some 20 years of age. She is the beauty and the glory of Bayou boeuf. She owns about 100 working hands, besides a great many houses servants, yard boys, and young children. Her brother-in-law, who resides on the adjoining estate, is her general agent. She is beloved by all her slaves, and good reason indeed have they to be thankful that they have fallen into such gentle hands. Nowhere on the Bayou are there such feasts, such merry making, as at that young Madam McCoy's. Thither, more than to any other place, do the old and the young for miles around love to repair in the time of the Christmas holidays; for nowhere else can they find such delicious repasts; nowhere else can they hear a voice speaking to them so pleasantly. No one is so well beloved--no one fills so large a space in the hearts of 1000 slaves, as young Madam McCoy, the orphan mistress of the old Norwood estate.

On my arrival at her place, I found a two or three hundred had assembled. The table was prepared in a long building, which she had erected expressly for her slaves to dance in. It was covered with every variety of food the country afforded, and was pronounced by general acclamation to be the rarest of dinners. Roasted Turkey, pig, chicken, duck, and all kinds of meat, baked, boiled, and broiled, formed a line the whole length of the extended table, while the vacant spaces were filled with tarts, jellies, and frosted cake, and pastry of many kinds. The young mistress walked around the table, smiling and saying a kind word to each one, and seemed to enjoy the scene exceedingly.

When the dinner was over the tables were removed to make room for the dancers. I tuned my violin and struck up a lively air; While some joined in a nimble reel, others padded and saying they're simple but melodious songs, filling the great room with music mingled with the sound of human voices and the clatter of many feet.

In the evening the mistress returned, and stood in the door along time, looking at us. She was magnificently arrayed. Her dark hair and eyes contrasted strongly with her clear and delicate complexion. Her form was slender but commanding, and her movement was a combination of unaffected dignity and grace. As she stood there, clad in her rich apparel, her face animated with pleasure, I thought I had never looked upon a human being half so beautiful. I dwell with delight upon the description of this fair and gentle lady, not only because she inspired me with emotions of gratitude and admiration, but because I would have the reader understand that all slave owners on Bayou booth are not like Epps or Tibeats or Jim Burns. Occasionally can be found, rarely it may be, indeed, a good man like William Ford, or an Angel of kindness like young Mistress McCoy.

14—ALBION

The transition was over, So it was said. The conventions had met in the various states, and in a marvelously short time had submitted constitutions which had been ratified by vote of the people. Officers had been chosen under them, they had been approved by the Congress of the nation as required by law, legislatures had met, senators and representatives in Congress had been chosen, the presidential election had taken place, and the Republican Party had achieved an overwhelmingly success. It was all over,--the war, reconstruction, the considerations of the old questions. Now all was peace and harmony. The South must take care of itself now. The nation had done its part: it had freed of the slaves, given them the ballot, opened the courts

to them, and put them in the way of self-protection and self-asser-
tion. The "root-hog-or –die" policy of the great apostle of the instan-
taneous transformation era became generally prevalent. The nation
heaved a sigh of relief. For three quarters of a century the South had
been the older man of the sea to the young Republic: by a simple trick
of political ledgermain he was now got rid of forever. No wonder the
Republic breathed freely! Yankee-land could now bend its undivided
energies to its industries and commerce. The South would take care of
itself, manage its own affairs, look after its own interest. The nation
was safe. It had put down rebellion, disbanded its armies, patched up
its torn map. The Republican Party had accomplished a great mission.
It had promised to put down rebellion, and had done so. It had guar-
anteed freedom to the slave, and had redeemed its promise. There was
nothing more to be done until, in the fullness of time, new issues,
should arise, based on new thoughts, new ideas, and new interests.

This is what the wise man said. But the fool looked on with anxious forebodings, and wrote to his old tutor gloomily of the future
that seemed so bright to others:

WARRINGTON, Dec. 10, 1868.

To DR. E. MARTIN.

My dear old Friend, — Your kind and welcome letter, so full
of congratulations and bright anticipations, was duly received, and
for it I render thanks. Must I confess it, however? It impresses me
with a feeling of sadness. The state of affairs which you picture does
not exist at the South; and the bright anticipations which you base
upon mistaken premises have, in my opinion, little chance of fulfillment. The freedman is just as impotent now of all power of self-protection as he was before the ballot was given him, — nay, perhaps
more so, as an unskilled person may injure himself with the finest of
Damascus blades. Pray keep in your mind my former classification. Of
every hundred of the blacks, ninety-five at least can not read or write,
ninety-five are landless, and at least eighty have not sufficient to subsist themselves for thirty days without the aid of those who are op-

posed to them in political thought with intensity of prejudice you can not begin to understand. These constitute three-fourths of the Republican party of the South. Of the remainder (the whites), twenty-four out of every hundred can not read their ballots ; and fifty-five or sixty of the same number are landless, being mere day-laborers, or at least renters, " crappers " as they are called here.

So that of this party, to whom the wise men of the North have given power, from whom they expect all but impossible things, three-fourths can not read or write, five-sevenths are landless, two-thirds are utterly impoverished, and nearly the whole is inexperienced in the conduct of public affairs. Yet upon this party the nation has rolled the burden of restoration, reconstruction, re-organization! That it will fail is as certain as the morrow's sunrise. For three years the nation has had this problem on the heads and hearts of its legislators, and has not made one step towards its solution. The highest wisdom, the greatest gravity, the profoundest knowledge, and that skill which comes only from experience, are indispensably necessary to this task. It is given into the hands of weaklings ; while the great country, whose interest, prosperity, and good faith, are all involved in securing the liberty conferred by the war, and in so organizing these new constituent elements that they shall hereafter be a source of strength, and not danger, — this country stands off, and says, " I will not touch one of the least of these burdens with my little finger. The South must take care of itself."

My dear old friend, it can not be done. The experiment must fail ; and, when it does fail, it will involve us all — us of the South, I mean in ruin ; but the North, and especially the Republican party of the North, will be responsible for this ruin, for its shame and its loss, for the wasted opportunity, and, it may be, for consequent peril. Of course I shall share it. The North would not see the fact that war did not mean regeneration, nor perform the duty laid upon it as a conqueror.

In fact, my dear doctor, I began seriously to fear that the North lacks virility. The cowardly shirking of responsibility, this pandering to sentimental whimsicality is, this snuffling wine about peace and conciliation, is sheer weakness. The north is simply a conqueror; and, if the result she fought for are to be secured, she must rule as a conqueror. Suppose the South had been triumphant, and had overwhelmed and determined to hold the north? Before now, a thoroughly organized system of provincial government would have been securely established. There would have been no hesitation, no subterfuge, no pretence of restoration because of the South are born rulers,--aggressives, who, having made-up their minds to attain a certain end, adopt the means most likely to secure it. In this the north fails. She hesitates, halters, shirks.

There is another danger. Rebellion has ended without punishment. It is true the South has lost,-- lost her men, her money, her slaves; but that was only a gambler's stake, the hazard placed upon the dice. There was talk of "making treason odious". How that result should be accomplished was a serious question; but how to make it honorable, I feel we have found as an easy matter to demonstrate.

As I have said, the party, if it may so be called, to whom the mighty task of rehabilitation has been assigned, must fail at the South. Already we hear the threat from the highest seats in the hostile camps, "Just wait until the Blue Coats are gone, and we will make Sodom and Gomorrah more tolerable than these States to Republicans !" They will do it too. They have the power, the intellect, the organizing capacity, the determined will. Our numbers only make us a cumbrous rope, of sand. Weak, incoherent particles are not made strong by mere multiplication. In the struggle against us, the most reckless and unworthy of those who led in the war will again come to the front. Their success will make them the heroes of the people, and they will win place and honor thereby. It will result that turbulent, ambitious men will hereafter say that the road to honor, renown, fame, and power, in our nation, lies through the Traitor's Gate." Burr and his coadjutors won only shame by their attempt to destroy the nation. Davis, Lee, and their compatriots have already won a distinction and eminence they could not have hoped for had they remained peaceful citizens of the Republic. They are destined to achieve far greater honor. From this day the prestige of the Federal soldier will begin to wane throughout the land. In the course of another decade, one will almost be ashamed to confess that he wore the blue. On the other hand, the glory of the Confederate leader will hourly wax greater and brighter. The latter has a people devoted and steadfast, to who pride, even in defeat, be can appeal with certainty of receiving an unshrinking response. The former has a country debauched by weak humanitarianisms, more anxious to avoid the appearance of offending its enemies than desirous of securing its own power or its own ends. These men who have led in the Rebellion will not be slow to perceive and take advantage of their opportunity and other generations following them will note the fact that the sure. safe, and brilliant road to fame and success is an armed rebellion against existing powers. You may think me discouraged and morbid: but mark my words, old friend, we have sown to the wind, and shall reap the whirlwind.

Yours Truly
Comfort Servose

15--CORNELIA

I now saw a good deal of my neighbors, for I was a social being. Sometimes I would divert myself with "Aunt Fanny," a servant grown too old to work, her rustic spinning-wheel, and her stories. Her house of two rooms, which she shared with another colored family, was in the back yard, just across the road from the quarters. All elderly negroes were called aunt and uncle by the younger ones instead of Mr. and Mrs. before the war and for some time after, though after the war they laid claims to surnames; the white people called them aunt and uncle according to the more or less respect they had for them.

A wood fire nearly always burned on her capacious hearth ; a black pot hung from the crane in the center. In the forenoon a cabbage and a piece of pork were likely boiling together in the pot for a twelve o'clock dinner ; the potato-bread baking in a skillet with a lid, red coals kept above and below it until it was baked. Then "Aunt Fanny" raked out some hot ashes and covered up her ash-cake, which she had prepared and wrapped in two damp cabbage leaves, and cooked it until it was a golden brown.

While the pot was boiling and the other victuals cooking she spun wool (to amuse herself) shorn from my father's Southdowns, for winter stockings; would let me try my hand at spinning, but it was more interesting to watch than to do. During her spinning she told tales of what happened in " ole times," full of ghosts and " speerits."

Aunt Matilda (still more superannuated) sometimes hobbled in, leaning on a stick, to take potluck, with a pipe of tobacco between her gums, and tell how " the pertaters whar she come from in Africa were as big as borrels," though she did not mention the size of the barrel ; and how my maternal great-grandfather, of Charleston, South Carolina, had such "bootiful" carpets the feet would sink to the ankles.

She was a good old soul. She loved my grandfather, and always cried when she looked at his portrait, which she sometimes asked to see. At his death she was left to my mother, and proved to be a most faithful servant.

15-- ALBION

I am indebted to Mr. Henry B Northup and others for many of the particulars contained in this chapter.

The letter written by Bass, directed to Parker and Perry, and which was deposited in the post office in Marksville on the 15th day of August, 1852, arrived at Saratoga in the early part of September. Sometime previous to this, Anne had removed to Glens Falls, Warren County, where she had a charge of the kitchen in Carpenters Hotel. She kept house, however, lodging with our children, and was only absent from them during such time as the discharge of her duties in the hotel required.

Messrs Parker and Perry, on receipt of the letter, forwarded immediately to Ann. On reading it the children were all excitement, and without delay hastened to the neighboring village of Sandy Hill, to consult Henry B Northup, and obtain his advice and assistance in the matter.

Upon examination, that gentleman found among the statutes of the state and act providing for the recovery of free citizens from slavery. It was passed May 14th, 1840, and is entitled "An act more effectually to protect the free citizens of this state from being kidnapped or reduced to slavery." It provides that it shall be the duty of the governor, upon the receipt of satisfactory information that any free citizen or inhabitant of this state, is wrongfully held in another state or territory of the United states, upon the allegation or pretense that such person is a slave, or by color of any usage or rule of law is deemed or taken to be a slave, to take such measures to procure the restoration of such person to liberty, as he shall deem necessary. And to that end, he is authorized to appoint an employee an agent, and directed to furnish him with such credentials and instructions as will be likely to accomplish the object of his appointment. It requires the agent so appointed to proceed to collect the proper proof to establish the right of such person to his freedom; to perform such journeys, take such measures, institute such legal proceedings etcetera as may be necessary to return such person to this state, and charges all expenses incurred in carrying the act into effect upon money's not otherwise appropriated in the treasury.

It was necessary to establish 2 facts to the satisfaction of the governor's: first, that I was a free citizen of New York; And secondly that I was wrongfully held in bondage. As to the first point, there was no difficulty, all the older inhabitants in the vicinity being ready to testify to it. The second point arrested entirely upon the letter to Parker and Perry, written in an unknown hand, and upon the letter penned on board the brig Orleans, which, unfortunately had been mislaid or lost.

Memorial was prepared, directed to his excellently, Governor Hunt, setting forth her marriage, my departure to Washington 's city; the receipt of the letters; That I was a free citizen, and such other facts as were deemed important, and was signed and verified by Anne accompany this memorial were several affidavits of prominent citizens of Sandy Hill and Fort Edward, corroborating fully the statements it contained, and also a request of several well known gentlemen to the governor, that Henry B Northup be appointed agent under the legislative act.

On reading the memorial and affidavits, His Excellency took a lively interest in the matter, and on the 23rd day of November, 1852, under the seal of the state, "constituted, appointed and employed Henry B Northup, Esquire, an agent, with full power to effect" my restoration, and at to take such measures as would be most likely to accomplish it, and instructing him to proceed to Louisiana with all convenient dispatch.

The pressing nature of Mr. Northup's professional and political engagements delayed his departure until December. On the 14th day of that month he left Sandy Hill, and proceeded to Washington. The honorable Pierre Soule, senator in Congress from Louisiana, Honorable Mr. Conrad, secretary of war, and a judge Nelson, of the Supreme Court of the United states, upon hearing a statement of the facts, and examining his Commission, and certified copies of the memorial and affidavits, furnished him with open letters to gentlemen in Louisiana, strongly urging their assistance in accomplishing the object of his appointment.

Senator Soule especially interested himself in the matter, insisting, in forceable language, that it was the duty and interest of every planter in his state to aid and restoring me to freedom, and trusted the sentiments of honor and justice in the bosom of every citizen of the Commonwealth which would enlist him at once in my behalf. Having obtained these valuable letters, Mr. Northup returned to Baltimore, and proceeded from thence to Pittsburgh. It was his original intention, under advice of friends at Washington, to go directly to New Orleans, and consult the authorities of that city. Providentially, however, on arriving at the mouth of Red River, he changed his mind. Had he continued on, he would not have met with Bass, in which case the search for me would probably have been fruitless.

Taking passage on the first steamer that arrived, he pursued his journey of a Red River, a sluggish, winding stream, flowing through a vast region of primitive forests and impenetrable swamps, almost wholly destitute of inhabitants. About 9:00 o'clock in the forenoon, January 1st, 1853, he left the Steamboat at Marksville, and proceeded directly to Marksville Courthouse, small village 4 miles in the interior.

From the fact that the letter to Messrs. Parker and Perry was postmarked at Marksville, it was supposed by him that I was in that place or its immediate vicinity. On reaching this town, he at once laid his business before the Honorable John P Waddill, a legal gentleman of distinction, and a man of fine genius and most noble impulses. After reading the letters and a documents presented him, and listening to a representation of the circumstances under which I had been carried away into captivity, Mr. Waddell at once proffered his services, and entered into the affair with great zeal and earnestness. He, in common with others of like elevated character, looked upon the kidnapper with a balance. The title of his fellow parishioners and clients to the property which constituted the larger proportion of their wealth, not only depended upon the good faith in which slave sales were transacted, but he was a man in whose honourable heart emotions of indignation were aroused by such an instance of injustice.

Marksville, although occupying A prominent position, and standing out in impressive italics on the map of Louisiana, his, in fact, but a small and insignificant hamlet. Aside from the Tavern, kept by a jolly and generous Boniface, the courthouse, inhabited by lawless cows and swine and the seasons of vacation, and a high gallows, with its diserviced rope dangling in the air, there is little to attract the attention of the stranger.

Solomon Northup was a name Mr. Waddill had never heard, but he was confident that if there was a slave bearing that appellation in Marksville or vicinity, his black boy Tom would know him. Tom was accordingly called, but in all his extensive circle of acquaintances there was no such personage.

The letter to Parker and Perry was dated at Bayou Boeuf. Add this place, therefore, the conclusion was, I must be sought. But here a difficulty suggested itself, of a very grave character indeed. Bayou Beouf, At its nearest point, was 23 miles distant, and was the name applied to the section of country extending between 50 and 100 miles, on both sides of that stream. Thousands and thousands of slaves resided upon its shores, the remarkable richness and fertility of the soil having attracted thither a great number of planters. The information in the letter was so vague and indefinite as to render it difficult to conclude upon any specific course of proceeding. It was finally determined, however, has the only plan that presented any prospect of success, that Northup and the brother of Woodill, a student in the office of the latter, should repair to the Bayou, and traveling up one side and down the other its whole length, inquire at each plantation for me. Mr. Waddill tendered the use of his carriage, and it was definitely arranged that they should start upon the excursion early Monday morning.

It will be seen at once that this course, in all probability, would have resulted unsuccessfully. It would have been impossible for them to have gone into the fields and examine all the gangs at work. They were not aware that I was known only as Platt; and had they inquired of Epps himself, he would have stated a truly that he knew nothing of Solomon Northup.

The arrangement being adopted, however, there was nothing further to be done until Sunday had elapsed. The conversation between Messrs Northup and Waddell, in the course of the afternoon, turned upon New York politics.

"I can scarcely comprehend the nice distinctions and shades of political parties in your state," observed Mr. Waddill. "I read of soft shells and hard shells, hunkers and barnburners, woolly heads and silvergrays, and am unable to understand the precise difference between them. Pray what is it?"

Mr. Northup, refilling his pipe, entered into quite an elaborate narrative of the origin of the various sections of parties, and concluded by saying there was another party in New York, known as free soilers or abolitionists. "You have seen none of those in this part of the country, I presume?" Mr. Northup remarked.

"Never, but one," answered Waddill, laughingly. "We have one here in Marksville, an eccentric creature, who preaches abolitionism as vehemently as any fanatic at the north. He is a generous, inoffensive man, but always maintaining the wrong side of an argument. It affords us a deal of amusement. He is an excellent mechanic, and almost indispensable in this community. He is a Carpenter. His name is Bass"

Some further good-natured conversation was had at the expense of Bass' peculiarities, when Waddill all at once fell into a reflective mood, and asked for the mysterious letter again.

"Let me see—l-e-t m-e s-e-e!" He repeated, thoughtfully to himself, running his eyes over the letter once more. " 'Bayou Boeuf August 15.' August 15-- postmarked here. 'He that is writing for me—' where did bass work last summer?" He inquired, turning suddenly to his brother. His brother was unable to inform him, but rising, left the office, and soon returned with the intelligence that "bass worked last summer somewhere on Bayou Boeuf."

"He is the man," bringing down his hand emphatically on the table, "who can tell us all about Solomon Northup," exclaimed Waddill.

Bass was immediately searched for, but could not be found. After some inquiry, it was ascertained he was at the landing on Red River. Procuring A conveyance, young Waddill and Northup were not long in traversing the few miles to the latter place. On their arrival, bass was found, just on the point of leaving, to be absent A fortnight or more. After an introduction, Northup begged at the privilege of speaking to him privately a moment. They walked together towards the river, when the following conversation ensued:

" Mr. Bass," said Northup, "Mr. Waddill told me to ask you if you were on Bayou Boeuf last August?"

"Yes, Sir, I was there in August," was the reply.

"Did you write a letter for a colored man at that place to some gentleman in Saratoga Springs?"

"Excuse me Sir, Sir, if i say that is none of your business," answered Bass, stopping and looking his interrogator searchingly in the face.

"Perhaps I am rather hasty, Mr. Bass; I beg your pardon; but I have come from the state of New York to accomplish the purpose the writer of a letter dated the 15th of August, postmarked at Marksville, had in view. Circumstances have led me to think that you are perhaps the man who wrote it. I am in search of Solomon Northup. If you know him, I beg you to inform me frankly where he is, and I assure you the source of any information you may give me shall not be divulged, if you desire it it not to be."

A long time Bass looked his new acquaintance steadily in the eyes, without opening his lips. He seemed to be doubting in his own mind if there was not an attempt to practice some deception upon him. Finally he said, deliberately--

"I have done nothing to be ashamed of. I am the man who wrote the letter. If you have come to rescue Solomon Northup, I am glad to see you."

"When did you last see him, and where is he?" Northup inquired.

"I last saw him Christmas, a week ago today. He is the slave of Edwin Epps, a planter on Bayou Boeuf, Near Holmesville. He is not known as Solomon Northup; He is called Platt."

The secret was out--the mystery was unraveled. Through the thick, black cloud, amid whose dark and dismal shadows I had walked 12 years, broke the star that was to light me back to liberty. All mistrust and hesitation were soon thrown aside, and the two men conversed long and freely upon the subject uppermost in their thoughts. Bass expressed the interest he had taken in my behalf--his intention of going north in the spring, and a declaring that he had resolved to accomplish my emancipation, if it were in his power. He described the commencement and progress of his acquaintance with me, and listened with eager curiosity to the account given him of my family, and the history of my early life. Before separating, he drew a map of the Bayou on a strip of paper with a piece of red chalk, showing the locality of Epps' plantation, And the road leading most directly to it.

15—ALBION

It was in the winter of 1868-69, therefore, when the wise men were jubilant over the success of the Great Experiment: when it was said that already Reconstruction had been an approved success, the

traces of the war been blotted out, and the era of the millennium anticipated, — that a little company of colored men came to the Fool
one day and one of them, who acted as spokesman, said, —

" What's dis we hear, Mars Kunnel, 'bout de Klux ? "

"The what ? " he asked.

" De Klux — de Ku-Kluckers dey calls demselves."

" Oh! the Ku-Klux, Ku-Klux-Klan, K. K. K.'s, you mean."

" Yes : dem folks what rides about at night a-pesterin' pore colored
people, an' a-pertendin' to be jes from hell, or some ob de battle-fields
ob ole Virginny."

" Oh, that's all gammon ! There is nothing in the world in it, —
nothing at all. Probably a parcel of boys now and then take it into
their heads to scare a few colored people but that's all. It is mean and
cowardly, but nothing more. You needn't have any trouble about it,
boys."

" An' you tink dat's all, Kunnel ? "

All ? Of course it is 1 What else should there be ? "

" I dunno, Mars Kunnel," said one.

" You don't tink dey's ghostses, nor noting ob dat sort ? asked another.

" Think! I know they are not."

" So do I," growled one of their number who had not spoken before, in a tone of such meaning that it drew the eyes of the Fool upon
him at once.

" So your mind's made up on that point too, is it, Bob ? he asked
laughingly.

"I know dey's not ghosts, Kunnel. I wish ter God dey was," was the
reply.

"Why, what do you mean, Bob? " asked the colonel in surprise.

.

"Will you jes help me take off my shirt, Jim ? " said Bob meaningly,
as he turned to one of those with him.

The speaker was taller than the average of his race, of a peculiarly jetty complexion, broad-shouldered, straight, of compact and powerful build. His countenance, despite its blackness. was sharply cut ; his head well shaped ; and his whole appearance and demeanor marked him as a superior specimen of his race. Servosse had seen him before, and knew him well as an industrious and thrifty blacksmith, living in a distant part of the county, who was noted as being one of the most independent and self-reliant of his people in all political as well as pecuniary matters, — Bob Martin by name.

When his clothing had been removed, he turned his back towards the Fool, and, glancing over his shoulder, said coolly, —

" What d'ye tink ob dat, Kunnel ? "

" My God ! " exclaimed the Fool, starting back in surprise and horror. " What does this mean, Bob ? "

" Seen de Kluckers, sah," was the grimly laconic answer.

The sight which presented itself to the Fool's eyes was truly terrible. The broad muscular back, from the nape down to and below the waist, was gashed and marked by repeated blows. Great furrows were plowed in the black integument, whose greenly-livid lips were drawn back, while the coagulated fibrine stretched across, and mercifully protected the lacerated flesh. The whole back was livid and swollen, bruised as if it had been brayed in a mortar. Apparently, after having cut the flesh with closely-laid welts and furrows, sloping downward from the left side towards the right, with that peculiar skill in castigation which could only be obtained through the abundant opportunity for severe and deliberate flagellation which prevailed under the benign auspices of slavery, the operator had changed his position, and scientifically cross-checked the whole. That he was an expert whose skill justified Bob's remark —" Nobody but an ole oberseer ebber dun dat, Kunnel " — was evident even on a casual inspection. The injury which the man had sustained, though extensive and severe, was not dangerous to one of his constitution and hardened physique. To the eye of the northern man who gazed at it, however, unused as are all his computers to witness the effects of severe whipping, it seemed horrible beyond the power of words to express. He did not reflect that the African could have had none of that sense of indignity and degradation with which the Caucasian instinctively regards the application of the emblem of servility, and that he was but fulfilling the end of his dusky being and submitting to such castigation.

Editor—Bob explains his whipping:

"Long a while back — p'raps five or six months —I refused ter du some work fer Michael Anson or his boy, 'cause dey'd run up quite a score at de shop, an' allers put me off when I wanted pay. I couldn't work jes fer de fun ob scorin' it down : so I quit. It made smart ob talk. Folks said I waz gettin' too smart fer a nigger, an' sech like ; but I kep right on; tole 'em, I waz a free man, — not born free, but made free by a miracle, — an' I didn't propose ter do any man's work fer noffin'. Most everybody hed somefin' to say about it ; but it didn't seem ter hurt my trade very much. I jes went on gittin' all I could do, an' sometimes moah. I s'pose I acted pretty independent : I felt so, anyhow. I staid at home, an' axed nobody any favors. I know'd der wa'n't a better blacksmif in de country, an' ought I hed tings jes' ez good ez I wanted 'em. When der come an election, I sed my say, did my own votin', an' tole de oder colored people dey waz free, an' hed a right ter du de same. Det's bad doctrine up in our country. De white folks don't like ter hear it, and 'specially don't like ter hear a nigger say it. Dey don't mind 'bout our gittin' on ef dey hey a mortgage, so't de 'arnin's goes into dar pockets ; nor 'bout our votin', so long ez we votes ez dey tells us. Dat's dare idea uv liberty fer a nigger.

"Well here a few weeks ago, I foun' a board stuck up on my shop one mornin'; wid dese words on to it : —

BOB MARTIN. - You're gettin' too dam smart ! The white folks round Burke's Cross-Roads don't want any sech smart niggers round dar. You'd better git, er you'll hev a call from de

" K. K. K.'

Editor—It was not just blacks. Those whites who sympathized with the free slaves were also subject to terror. The letter below is an example.

Here is one from our old friend, Dr. Garnett :

MY DEAR FRIEND,- It seems that it is even worse to be a native ' here, and to the manner born,' if one presumes to disagree with his neighbors, than to be a carpet-bagger,' such as you are called ; for the evil of which I lately warned you has befallen me. Night before last the Ku-Klux came. I had never believed they would attack me; but I had not neglected making some simple and obvious precautions for such a contingency. You know my house is a perfect blockhouse any-how. It was first made of hewed logs, closely chinked, and afterwards weather-boarded, and ceiled with inch lumber on the inside. Since the K. K. K. came in vogue, I had put heavy wooden bars across the doors, and added heavy inside shutters of inch boards to the windows, with little loop-holes at the side in case of attack. it was a bright night, not moonlight, but starry. I had been out late ; and, after getting supper, we were having family prayers before retiring. We always lock every thing about the house at dark. My wife and daughter Louisa were all that were at home with me. During the prayer, my wife, who was kneeling nearest the front-door, came over, and, touching me on the shoulder, said, ' They have comae!'

I knew to whom she referred at once; and, adding one brief peti-tion for help, I closed my prayer. There were evident sounds of foot-steps crowding the little front porch by that time. Then there came a rap on the door, and a demand that it be opened. This I refused to do, ordered them to leave my premises, and warned them that they remained at their peril.

I gave my wife and daughter each a revolver. They are both deli-cate women, as you know; but they have learned to handle fire-arms for just such an occasion, and they did not quail. By this time those outside were assailing both the front and back doors. I looked out at one of my little port-holes, and could see them standing about the porch. A good many shots were fired also at the doors and windows.

I thought I ought not to wait any longer; and so, with a prayer for myself and for my enemies outside, I put my gun to the port-hole, glanced along it, and pulled the trigger. There was a shriek, a groan, and a hurrying of feet away from the door. When the smoke cleared away, I thought I could see one of those cloaked and hooded forms lying across the path before the house. I dared not go out to proffer aid or bring him in, lest the others should be in ambush, and fall upon me. My sight is not first-rate ; but Louisa said she could see them lurking about the fence and bushes before the house. After this the attack seemed to cease. I was on the alert, however, believing them to be as ruthless and reckless as wild Indians on the war-path. Presently, watching towards the front, I saw two figures come softly and cautiously up the road, and after a time into the yard. They stole along from tree to shrub like murderous redskins, and I was about to fire on them, when they stopped at the body lying across the path. They consulted _a moment, evidently examining the body; then one went off, and led a horse up to the gate. They lifted up the body, taking it between them to the horse, and with no little difficulty placed it across the saddle, and lashed it around the horse; then they rode off, and, as they passed up the hill by the Widow Johnson's, we could hear that there were a good many. We kept watch until morning, but neither saw nor heard any thing more of them. As soon as it was good light, I went out and examined the path. There was a great pool of blood, which had also dripped along the path to the gate, and beyond that in the road. Getting on my horse, and taking my gun, I followed the trail of blood until it crossed the Little Rocky River, after which I lost it.

" I have strong suspicions as to who were in the party. Today there was a funeral down in the Fork, of a man who was kicked by a mule yesterday morning. The undertaker who buried him said he was already laid out when he came to the house, and some men who were there insisted on putting him in the coffin. When the undertaker was putting the cover down, however, he got a chance to put his hand down on the head of the corpse. He says, if that man was killed by a mule, it must have been a remarkably tall one. It seems impossible ; yet I can not but suspect that this man was the leader, and that he died by my hand. Strange as it seems now, I have often met him at the Lord's table. He was a very active member of the church, and was a superintendent of a sabbath school.

I have even a stranger fact to record. You remember my daughter's hair was a soft light brown. It was so the night of the attack. In the morning it was streaked with gray, and now it is almost as silvery as mine. She is but twenty-three. Ah these villains have a terrible sight of crime and agony to answer for. I hear they are raiding all about the country, whipping and mutilating without restraint. Can nothing be done? Is our government so weak that it can not protect its citizens at home?

Yours,

" GEORGE D. GARNETT

16

16—CORNELIA

The country now was beautiful with its new foil age, and the air sweet with the wholesome odors of freshly plowed fields and growing things. My greatest diversion at this time was horseback riding. My girlfriends often joined me by appointment in the morning, or some friend of the other sex in the afternoon; Otherwise I had Sancho put on his Sunday suit and follow behind. He was a saucy fellow. If you gave him an inch he took an ell [about 45 inches], but he never spoke of his "maw" and "paw" like so many of the other negroes; it was "mammy" and pappy, nor did he mention his friends as "gentl'men" and "ladies" as did the others, to help them to realize their freedom.

After the war, public schools sprang up here and there for the negroes, but Sancho did not avail himself of these advantages, as he did not like application. I frequently told him his grammar was atrocious.

" Now, young Mistis," he would say, " tain't no use usin' dem hif'lutin' words to me, deh jess goes in one yeah en comes out t'otheh."

Picnics were in vogue now on the shady banks of some Bayou, where hours were spent in catching crayfish and afterward enjoying the delightful bisque every cook in that region knows so well how to make.

Now, I pray fish is a sly thing. When you think you have him almost on the shore he often wiggles back into the water--hence sancho and the net were necessary. Crayfish pinch unless one knows how to manipulate them. They pinched him often, he teased them so much. The excitement of it must have sharpened his wits, for his remarks were unique and to the point.

179

Though my life was so full of pleasure, like most of my girl companions I did some of my plain sewing and sometimes made a party dress, or visiting dress; frequently rigged up a coquettish hat when I wanted something different. If the maids did not appear I looked after the rooms, and once, went about 14, I've volunteered to cook dinner.

As a child I'd liked the culinary department and hung around Ellen in the kitchen very much, which bothered her no doubt, as she frequently threatened to throw the dish rag on me if I did not get out of her way. I found out I had learned something, and my dinner was pronounced very nice. Ellen was sick, and Martha western take her place till she recovered, I heard heard that Martha was roguish, and I asked James Madison if it was true. He said well marm, I don't know exactly about that and wouldn't like to say pointedly but how some ever eyes heard among them that knows that she is powerful thrifty

I now saw a good deal of my neighbours, for I was a social being. Sometimes I would divert myself with "Aunt Fanny", a servant grown too old to work, her rustic spinning-wheel and her stories. Her house of two rooms, which she shared with another colored family, was in the backyard, just across the road from the quarters. All elderly negroes were called aunt and uncle by the younger ones instead of Mr. and Mrs. before the war and for some time after, though after the war they laid claims to surnames; the white people called them aunt and uncle according to the more or less respect they had for them.

A wood fired nearly always burned on her [Aunt Fanny's] capacious hearth; A black pot hung from the crane in the center. In the forenoon a cabbage and a piece of pork were likely boiling together in the pot for a 12:00 dinner; the potato bread baking in a skillet with a lid, red coals kept above and below it until it was baked. Then Aunt Fanny raked out some hot ashes and covered up her ash cake which she had prepared and wrapped in two damp cabbage leaves, and cooked it until it was a golden brown.

While the part was boiling and other victuals cooking she spun wool (to amuse herself) shorn from my father's Southdowns, for winter stockings; She would let me try my hand at spinning, but it was more interesting to watch than to do. During her spinning she told tales of what happened in old times full of ghosts and spirits.

She was a good old soul. She loved my grandfather, and always cried when she looked at his portrait, which she sometimes asked to see. At his death she was left to my mother, and proved to be a most faithful servant.

Beth still lives in her cabin at the White Castle, but Aunt Fanny and Aunt Matilda have been gathered to their fathers for several years, and some of the family went to the burials. My old mammy followed me to my new home, to look after me—and the children later—but I take care that she has not much to do, and as long as I have a home she shall be carefully looked after. She still loves to read the Bible, but her eyes are getting dim. Once a day I read her a chapter, and explain it to her to the best of my ability. And I trust I shall meet her in the world above, for though she is not as fair as I am, it must be that it is the pure heart that will shine, and make the face radiant in that unknown realm which giveth the peace which passeth understanding.

16-- SOLOMON

Northup and his young companion returned to Marksville, where it was determined to commence legal proceedings to test the question of my right to freedom. I was made plaintiff, Mr. Northup acting as my guardian, and Edwin Epps defendant. The process to be issued was in the nature of replevin [a writ to reclaim property], directed to the sheriff of the parish, commanding him to take me into custody, and detain me until the decision of the court. By the time the papers were duly drawn up, it was 12:00 o'clock at night--too late to obtain the necessary signature of the judge, who resided some distance out of town. Further business was therefore suspended until Monday morning.

Everything, apparently, was moving along swimmingly, until Sunday afternoon, when Waddill called at Northup's room to express his apprehension of difficulties that they had not expected to encounter. Bass had become alarmed, and had placed his affairs in the hands of a person at the landing, communicating to him his intention of leaving the state. This person had betrayed at the confidence reposed in him to a certain extent, and a rumor began to float about the town, that the stranger at the hotel, who had been observed in the company of lawyer Waddill, was after one of old Epps' slaves, over on the Bayou. Epps was known at Marksville, having frequent occasion to visit that place during the session of the courts, and the fear entertained by Northrup's advisor was, that intelligence would be conveyed to him in the night, giving him an opportunity of secreting me before the arrival of the sheriff.

This apprehension had the effect of expediting matters considerably. The sheriff, who lived in One Direction from the village, was requested to hold himself in readiness immediately after midnight, while the judge was informed he would be called upon at the same time. It is but justice to say, that at the authorities and Marksville cheerfully rendered all the assistance in their power.

Has soon after midnight has bail could be perfected, and the judge's signature obtained, a carriage, containing Mr. Northup and the sheriff, driven by the landlord 's son, rolled rapidly out of the village of Marksville, on the road towards Bayou Boeuf.

It was supposed that Epps would contest the issue involving my right to liberty, and it therefore suggested itself to Mr. Northup, that the testimony of the sheriff, describing my first meeting with the former, might perhaps become material on the trial. It was accordingly arranged during the ride, that, before I had an opportunity of speaking to Mr. Northup, the sheriff should propound to me certain questions agreed upon, such as the number and names of my children, the name of my wife before marriage, of places I knew at the north, and so forth. If my answers corresponded with a statements given him. The evidence must necessarily be considered conclusive.

At length, shortly after Epps had left the field, with the consoling assurance that he would soon return and warn warm us, as was stated in the conclusion of the preceding chapter, they came in sight of the plantation, and discovered us at work. Alighting from the carriage, and directing the driver to proceed to the great house, with instructions not to mention to anyone the object of their errand until they met again, Northup and the sheriff turned from the highway, and came towards us across the cotton field. We observed them, on looking up at the carriage--one several rods in advance of the other. It was a singular and unusual thing to see white men approaching us in that manner, and especially at that early hour in the morning, and Uncle Abram and Patsy made some remarks, expressive of their astonishment. Walking up to Bob, the sheriff inquired:

"Where's the boy they call Platt?"

"Thar he is, Massa," answered Bob, pointing to me, and twitching off his hat.

I wondered to myself what business he could possibly have with me, and turning round, gazed at him until he had approached within a step. During my long residence on the Bayou, I had become familiar with the face of every planter within many miles; but this man was an utter stranger--certainly I had never seen him before.

"Your name is Platt, is it?" He asked

"Yes, master," I responded.

Pointing towards Northup, standing a few rods distant, he demanded—" do you know that man?"

I looked in the direction indicated, and as my eyes rested on his countenance, a world of images thronged my brain; a multitude of well-known faces—Anne's, and the dear children's, and my old dead father's; all the scenes and associations of childhood and youth; all the friends of other and happier days, appeared and disappeared, floating and floating like dissolving shadows before the vision of my imagination, until at last the perfect memory of the man recurred to me, and throwing up my hands towards Heaven, I exclaimed, in a voice louder than I could utter in a less exciting moment--

"Henry B Northup! Thank God--thank God!"

In an instant I comprehended the nature of his business, and felt that the hour of my deliverance was at hand. I started towards him, but the sheriff stepped before me.

"Stop a moment," said he; "have you any other name than Platt?"

"Solomon Northup is my name, master," I replied.

"Have you a family?" He inquired.

"I had a wife and three children."

"What were your children's names?"

"Elizabeth, Margaret and Alonzo."

"And your wife's name before her marriage?"

"Anne Hampton."

"Who married you?"

"Timothy Eddy, of Fort Edward."

"Where does that gentleman live?" Again pointing to Northup, who remained standing in the same place where I had first recognized him.

"He lives in Sandy Hill, Washington County, New York," was the reply.

He was proceeding to ask further questions, but I pushed past him, unable longer to restrain myself. I seized my old acquaintance by both hands. I could not speak. I could not refrain from tears.

"Sol," He said at length," I'm glad to see you."

I essayed to make some answer, but emotion choked all utterance, and I was silent. The slaves, utterly confounded, stood gazing upon the scene, their open mouths and rolling eyes indicating the utmost wonder and astonishment. For 10 years I had dwelt among them, in the field and in the cabin, born at the same hardships, partaken the same fare, mingled my griefs with theirs, participated in the same scanty joys; nevertheless, not until this hour, the last I was to remain among them, had the remotest suspicion of my true name, or the slightest knowledge of my real history, been entertained by any of them.

Not a word was spoken for several minutes, during which time I clung fast to Northup, looking up into his face, fearful I should awake and find it all a dream.

"Throw down that sack," Northup added, finally, "your cotton-picking days are over. Come with us to the man you live with."

I obeyed him, and walking between him and the sheriff, when you moved towards the great house. It was not until we had proceeded some distance that I had recovered to my voice sufficiently to ask if my family were all living. He informed me he had seen Anne, Margaret and Elizabeth but a short time previously; that Alonzo was still living, and all were well. My mother, however, I could never see again. As I began to recover in some measure from the sudden and great excitement which so overwhelmed me, I grew faint and weak, and so much it was with difficulty I could walk. The sheriff took hold of my arm and assisted me, or I think I should have fallen. As we entered the yard, Epps stood by the gate, conversing with the driver. That young man, faithful to his instructions, was entirely unable to give him the least information in answer to his repeated inquiries of what was going on. By the time we reached him he was almost as much amazed and puzzled as Bob or Uncle Abram.

Shaking hands with the sheriff, hand receiving an introduction to Mr. Northup, he invited them into the house, ordering me, at the same time, to bring in some wood. It was some time before I succeeded in cutting an armful, having, somehow, unaccountably lost the power of wielding the axe with any manner of precision. When I entered with it at last, the table was strewn with papers, from one of which Northup was reading. I was probably longer than necessity required, and placing the sticks upon the fire, being particular as to the exact position of each individual one of them. I heard the words, "the said Solomon Northup," and "the deponent further says," and "free citizen of New York," Repeated frequently, and from these expressions understood that the secret I had so long retained from master and mistress Epps, was finally developing. I lingered as long as prudence permitted, and was about leaving the room, when Epps inquired,

"Platt, do you know this gentleman?"

"Yes, master," I replied, "I have known him as long as I can remember."

"Where does he live?"

"He lives in New York."

"Did you ever live there?"

"Yes, master-- born and bred there."

"He was free, then. Now you damned, nigger," he exclaimed, "why did you not tell me that when I bought you?"

"Master Epps," I answered, in a somewhat different tone than the one in which I had been accustomed to address him—" Master Epps, you did not take the trouble to ask me; I told one of my owners--the man that kidnapped me--that I was free, and was whipped almost to death for it."

"It seems there has been a letter written for you by somebody. Now, who is it?" He demanded, authoritatively. I made no reply.

"I say, who wrote that letter?" He demanded again.

"Perhaps I wrote it myself," I said.

"You haven't been to Marksville post office and back before light, I know."

He insisted upon my informing him, and I insisted I would not. He made many vehement threats against the man, whoever he might be, and intimated the bloody and savage pensions he would wreak upon him, when he found him out. His whole manner and language exhibited a feeling of anger towards the unknown person who had written for me, and of fretfulness at the idea of losing so much property. Addressing Mr. Northup, He swore yeah if he had only had an hours' notice of his coming, he would have saved him the trouble of taking me back to New York; that he would have run me into the swamp, or some other place out of the way, where all the sheriffs on earth couldn't have found me.

I walked out into the yard, and was entering the kitchen door, when something struck me in the back. Aunt Phebe, he emerging from the back door of the great house with a pan of potatoes, had thrown one of them with unnecessary violence, thereby giving me to understand that she wished to speak to me a moment confidentially. Running up to me, she whispered in my ear with great earnestness,

"Lor a' mity, Platt! What d'ye think? Dem two men come after ye. Heard 'em tell massa you free--got wife and a tree children back thar whar you come from. Goin' wid 'em? Fool if ye don't--wish I could go," and Aunt Phebe ran on in this manner at a rapid rate.

Presently Mistress Epps made her appearance in the kitchen. She said many things to me, and I wondered why I had not told her who I was. She expressed her regret, complimenting me by saying she had rather lose any other servant on the plantation. Had a Patsey that day stood in my place, the measure of my mistress' joy would have over-flowed. Now there was no one left who could mend a chair or a piece of furniture--no one who was of any use about the house--no one who could play for her on the violin--and mistress Epps was actually affected to tears.

Epps had called to Bob to bring up his saddle horse. The other slaves, also, overcoming their fear of the penalty, had left their work and come to the yard. They were standing behind the cabins, out of sight of Epps. They beckoned me to come to them, and with all the ea-gerness of curiosity, excited to the highest pitch, conversed with and questioned me. If I could repeat the exact words they uttered, with the same emphasis--if I could paint it there several attitudes, and the expression of their countenances--it would be indeed an interesting picture. And their estimation, I had suddenly arisen to an immeasur-able height-- had become a being of immense importance.

The legal papers having been served, and arrangements made with Epps to meet them the next day at Marksville, Northup and the sheriff entered the carriage to return to the latter place. As I was about mounting to the driver's seat, the sheriff said I ought to bid Mr. and Mrs. Epps goodbye. I ran back to the Piazza where they were standing, and taking off my hat, said,

"Goodbye, missis."

"Goodbye, Platt," said Mrs. Epps, kindly.

"Goodbye, master."

"Ah! You damned nigger," muttered Epps, in a surly, malicious tone of voice, "you needn't feel so cussed tickled-- you ain't gone yet-- I'll see about this business at Marksville tomorrow."

I was only a "nigger" and knew my place, but felt as strongly as if I had been a white man, that it would have been an inward comfort, had I dared to have given him a parting kick. On my way back to the carriage, Patsey ran from behind a cabin and threw her arms around my neck.

"Oh, Platt," she cried, tears streaming down her face, "you're goin' to be free--you're goin' way off yonder, where we'll nebber see you anymore. You've saved me a good many whippins, Platt; I'm glad you're goin' to be free—but oh! De Lord, de Lord! What'll become of me?"

I disengaged myself from her, and entered the carriage. The driver cracked his whip and away we rolled. I looked back and saw Patsey, with drooping head, Half reclining on the ground; Mrs. Epps was on the Piazza; Uncle Abram, and Bob, and Wiley, and aunt Phoebe Stood by the gate, gazing after me. I waved my hand, but the carriage turned a bend of the Bayou, hiding them from my eyes forever.

We stopped a moment at Kerry sugar house, where a great number of slaves were at work, such an establishment being a curiosity to a northern man. Epps dashed to buy us on horseback at full speed--on the way, as we learned next day, to the pine woods to see William Ford, who had brought me into the country.

Tuesday, the 4th of January, Epps and his counsel, the honorable H Taylor, Northup, Waddill, the judge and sheriff of Avoyelles, and myself, met in a room in the village of Marksville. Mr. Northup stated the facts in regard to me, and presented his Commission, and the affidavits accompanying it. The sheriff described the scene in the cotton field. I was also interrogated at great length. Finally, Mr. Taylor assured his client that he was satisfied, and that litigation would not only be expensive, but utterly useless. In accordance with his advice, a paper was drawn up and signed by the proper parties, wherein Epps acknowledged he was satisfied of my right to freedom, and formerly surrendered me to the authorities of New York. It was also stipulated that it be entered of record in the recorder's office of Avoyelles.

Mr. Northup and myself immediately hastened to the landing, and taking passage on the first steamer that arrived, were soon floating down Red River, up which, with such desponding thoughts, I had been borne 12 years before.

16-- ALBION

Uncle Jerry had been noted for his openly expressed defiance of the Ku Klux, his boldness in denouncing them, and the persistency with which he urged the colored men of his vicinity to organize, and resist the aggressions of that body. In this he had been partially successful. A considerable number of the inhabitants of the colored suburb had armed themselves, had appointed a leader and lieutenants and agreed upon signals, on hearing which all were to rally for defense at certain designated points. He had infused into his duller minded associates the firm conviction which possessed himself,-- that it was better to die in resisting such oppression than to live under it. He had an idea that his race must commit in a sense, achieve its own liberty, establish its own manhood, by a stubborn resistance to aggression,--an idea which it is altogether probable would have been the correct and proper one, had not the odds of ignorance and prejudice been so decidedly against them.

Editor—The following is an account of the KKK's response to Uncle Jerry's impertinence.

On that night the little suburban village sank to its usual repose, after their laborers and cares which Saturday night imposes upon people of low degree. The bacon and meal for the next week had been
purchased, the clothes for the Morrow put in order, and preparations made for that Sunday dinner which the poorest colored family
manages to make a little better than the weekday meal. It was nearly
12:00 when all became silent; and the weary workers slept all the more
soundly for the six days labor of the week which was passed.

It was a chill, Jerry knight. A dry, harsh wind blew from the north.
The moon was at the full and shone clear and cold in the blue vault.

There was 1 shrill whistle, some noise of quietly moving horses;
and those who looked from their window saw a black gowned and
grimly masked horsemen sitting upon a draped horse at every corner
of the streets, and before each house,-- grim, silent, threatening.
Those who saw dear not move, or give any alarm. Instinctively they
knew that the enemy they had feared had come, had them in his
clutches, and would work his will of them, whether they resisted or
not. So, with the instinct of self preservation, all were silent--all sim-
ulated sleep.

Five, 10, 15 minutes the silent watch continued. A half hour passed,
and there had been no sound. Each masked century sat his horse as if
horse and rider were only some magic statuary with which the bleak
knight cheated the off frightened eyes. Then a whistle sounded on the
road toward Verdenton. The masked horsemen turned their horses
heads in that direction, and slowly and silently moved away.

Gathering in twos', they fell into ranks with the regularity and
ease of a practiced soldiery and, as they filed on towards Verdenton,
showed a cavalcade of several hundred strong; and upon one of the
foremost horses rode one with a strange figure lashed securely to him.

When the few who were awake in the little village found courage
to inquire as to what the silent enemy had done, they rushed from
house to house with chattering teeth and trembling limbs, only to find
that all were safe within, until they came to the house where old Un-

cle Jerry Hunt had been dwelling alone since the death of his wife six months before. The door was open.

The house was empty The straw mattress had been thrown from the bed, and the hempen cord on which it rested had been removed.

The sabbath-morrow was well advanced when the Fool was first apprised of the raid. He at once rode into the town, arriving there just as the morning services closed, and met the people coming along the streets to their homes. Upon the limb of a low-branching oak not more than forty steps from the Temple of Justice, hung the lifeless body of old Jerry. The wind turned it slowly to and fro. The snowy hair and beard contrasted strangely with the dusky pallor of the peaceful face, which seemed even in death to proffer a benison to the people of God who passed to and fro from the house of prayer, unmindful both of the peace which lighted the dead face, and of the rifled temple of the Holy Ghost which appealed to them for sepulture. Over all pulsed the sacred echo of the sabbath bells. The sun shone brightly. The wind rustled the autumn leaves. A few idlers sat upon the steps of the court-house, and gazed carelessly at the ghastly burden on the oak. The brightly-dressed church-goers enlivened the streets. Not a colored man was to be seen. All except the brown cadaver on the tree spoke of 'peace and prayer —a holy day among a godly people, with whom rested the benison of peace.

The Fool asked of some trusty friends the story of the night before. , With trembling lips one told it to him,

"I heard the noise of horses quiet and orderly, but many. Looking from the window in the clear moonlight, I saw horsemen passing down the street, taking their stations here and there, like guards who have been told off for duty, at specific points. Two stopped before my house, two opposite Mr. Haskin's, and two or three upon the corner below. They seemed to have been sent on before as a sort of picket-guard for the main body, which soon came in. I should say there were from a hundred to a hundred and fifty still in line. They were all masked, and wore black robes. The horses were disguised, too, by drapings. There were only a few mules in the whole company. They were good horses, though: one could tell that by their movements. Oh, it was a respectable crowd! No doubt about that, sir. Beggars don't ride in this country. I don't know when I have seen so many good horses together since the Yankee cavalry left here after the surrender. They were well drilled too. Plenty of old soldiers in that crowd. Why, every thing went just like clock-work. Not a word was said — just a few whistles given. They came like a dream, and went away like a mist. I thought we should have to fight for our lives; but they did not disturb any one here. They gathered down by the courthouse. I could not see precisely what they were at, but, from my back upper window, saw them down about the tree. After a while a signal was given, and just at that time a match was struck, and I saw a dark body swing down under the limb. I knew then they had hung somebody, but had no idea who it was. To tell the truth, I had a notion it was you, Colonel. I saw several citizens go out and speak to these men on the horses. There were lights in some of the offices about the courthouse, and in several of the houses about town. Every thing was as still as the grave, — no shouting or loud talking, and no excitement or stir about town. It was evident that a great many of the citizens expected the movement, and were prepared to co-operate with it by manifesting no curiosity, or otherwise endangering its success. I am inclined to think a good many from this town were in it. I never felt so powerless in my life. Here the town was in the hands of two or 300 armed and disciplined men, hidden from the eye of the law, and having friends and coworkers in almost every house. I knew that resistance was useless."

"But why," ask the fool, "has not the body been removed?"

"We have been thinking about it," was the reply; "but the truth is, it don't seem like a very safe business. And, after what we saw last night, no one feels like being the 1st to do what may be held in a front by those men. I tell you, Colonel, I went through the war, and saw as much danger as most men in it; but I would rather charge up the heights of Gettysburg again than to be the object of a raid by that crowd."

After some parlay, however, some colored men were found, and a little party made-up, who went out and saw the body of Uncle Jerry cut down, and laid upon a box to await the coming of the coroner, who had already been notified. The inquest developed only these facts, and the sworn jurors solemnly and honestly found the cause of death unknown. One of the colored men who had watched the proceedings gave utterance to the prevailing opinion, when he said,--

"It don't do for niggers to know too much! Dat's what ail Uncle Jerry!"

And indeed it did seem as if this case was one in which ignorance might have been bliss.

17

17-- CORNELIA

A small log of wood was slowly burning, one end on the homely iron dog, the other resting on the hearth of the great brick fireplace in a cabin which stood behind the fig orchard at the White Castle—a fence intervening. It was in the late spring, but when is it that a darky does not enjoy a blaze? The very crackle of the wood inspires comfort.

Elizabeth Flowers (familiarly called " Beth " by the inmates and the whole family connection of the mansion) was reclining in an antiquated wooden rocker, not feeling well this afternoon ; a many-colored kerchief on her head, a little red square shawl on her shoulders, over a calico waist. She was eating some wine jelly just brought her by Victoria. Victoria had received her name in memory of England's Queen, and had some of her kindness. "I tell you whut, Miss Victohia, dis iz good," looking at her admiringly and rubbing her thin stomach.

" How yeh does favor ole Marsteh, yeh grandpaw, en I likes to see it. When I wuz a young gal I wuz took, wid Nick, to be sold, en when Marsteh tole de man dat he settle on Nick caze he wuz big en strong, I got down on meh knees en beg him to buy me too. I wuz little en thin en wuzn't strong, but Marsteh tole de man to let me go 'long wid Nick, en I'ze been hyeh eveh since. Nick wuz drownded in de riber, yeh know, not long ago, but I had many a happy yeah wid him befo' dat, do'h wheneveh Nick sass me I got up en pound him wid meh fists, en he would jess laf', caze I wuz so little. I couldn' hurt him nohow. Miss Victohia, when yeh gits mah'ied dars nothin' like showin' de man yeh has some grit. Nick liked Miss Penelope, caze he say she made such purty rhymes. He would walk pas' de house on pu'pose when he see heh playin"roun', wid his net on he shouldeh, goin' fishin, en he'd say :

" Miss Penelope, whut's de matteh ?' den she'd say:

" De dog stuck his foot in de batteh!' [broad a].

" Nick come frum Fudginia, yeh know, en talk like dem fo'ks, en Miss Penelope would talk dat-away to match him. Some otheh time he'd hollo out :

" Miss Penelope, how are yeh to-day ?' she say :

" Vehy well, if meh hens would lay.'

" She had a little hen-house under a big tree near her maw's room. Nick he laf' en say :

" 'What are yeh goin' to do to-morrow ?' [he always said are instea of iz.] She answer back:

" Roll yeh in a wheel barrow' [broad a]. At dat Nick he mos' kill hisse'f laffin'—he wuz nigh seben foot high en she no bigger'n dis cheer Ize settin' in. Doh I never could do much at a time, I wuz a good nus' when fo'ks wuz sick, en in slave times I went to de hospital wid de docteh all de time to take his ordehs 'bout people whut wuz sick. De sick people always went to Marsteh fus', en he would feel deir pulse en tell 'em to come to me fur de med'cine. When yeh gran'maw had company en needed mor'n she already had. I used to make nic-nacs [delicacies] for heh. Sh en Mateh wuz mighty good; yeh gran'maw iz yet, but yeh gran'paw, iz gone whar de good fo'ks go. Yeh favors yeh gran'paw, en dat ketches meh eye. when yeh gran'paw ceasted yeh waz mos' too young to remembah, but he had de bigges' funeral yeh evah huyd tell on. De high en low, de rich en de po'. En dey tells me he built de bes' part o' de chu'ch whar yeh all goes Sundays, en mos' ob de pars'nage whar de minister's family stay, besides entertainin' all de Bishops en stray minisrehs whut come along.

17--SOLOMON

We left Washington on the 20th of January, and proceeding by way of Philadelphia, New York, and Albany, reached sandy hill in the night of the 21st. My heart overflowed with happiness as I looked around upon old familiar scenes, and found myself in the midst of friends of other days. The following morning I started, in company with several acquaintances, for Glens Falls, the residence of Anne and our children.

As I entered their comfortable cottage, Margaret was the first that met me. She did not recognize me. When I left her, she was but seven years old, a little prattling girl, playing with her toys. Now she was grown to womanhood--was married, with a bright eyed boy standing by her side. Not forgetful of his enslaved, unfortunate grandfather, she had named the child Solomon Northup Staunton. When told who I was, she was overcome with emotion, and unable to speak. Presently Elizabeth entered the room, and Anne came running from the hotel, having been informed of my arrival. They embraced me, and with tears flowing down their cheeks, hung upon my neck. But I draw a veil over a scene which can better be imagined than described. When the violence of our emotions has subsided to a sacred joy--when the household gathered around the fire, that sent out its warm and crackling comfort through the room, we conversed of the thousand events that had occurred--the hopes and fears, the joys and sorrows, the trials and the troubles we had each experienced during the long separation. Alonzo was absent in the western part of the state. The boy had written to his mother a short time previous, of the prospect of his obtaining sufficient money to purchase my freedom. From his earliest years, that had been the chief object of his thoughts and his ambition. They knew I was in bondage. The letter written on board the brig, and Clem Ray himself, had given them that information. But where I was, until the arrival of Bass's letter, was a matter of conjecture. Elizabeth and Margaret once returned from school--so an informed me-- weeping bitterly. On inquiring the cause of the children's sorrow, it was found that, while studying geography, their attention had been attracted to the picture of slaves working in the cotton field, and an overseer following them with his whip. It reminded them of the sufferings their father might be, and, as it happened, actually was, enduring in the South. Numerous incidents, such as these, were related--incidents showing they still held me in constant remembrance, but not, perhaps, of sufficient interest to the reader, to be recounted.

My narrative is at an end. I have no comments to make upon the subject of slavery. Those who read this book may form their own opinions of the "peculiar institution." What it may be in other states, I do not profess to know; what it is in the region of the Red River, is truly and faithfully delineated in these pages. This is no fiction, no exaggeration. If I have failed in anything, it has been in presenting to the reader too prominently the bright side of the picture. I doubt not hundreds have been as unfortunate as myself; That hundreds of free citizens have been kidnapped and sold into slavery, and are at this moment wearing out their lives on plantations in Texas and Louisiana. But I forbear. Chastened and subdued in spirit by the sufferings I have borne , and thankful to that good Being through whose mercy I have been restored to happiness and liberty, I hope henceforward to lead an upright though lowly life, and rest at last in the churchyard where my father sleeps.

17—Editor

Before this final passage, I ask that you contemplate what has transpired in these last 150 years. Slavery is gone, but vestiges remain. The United States of America has never been a homogeneous group of like-minded people. Never. Is that bad? Should we all be the same? And how would that sameness manifest itself? Who should decide? We can take a vote on the laws, but is it even possible to vote on who we are? I've always felt that the term "We The People" was a little unfortunate.

I grew up in a white suburb of Boston. Then, for two years, I went to engineering school in the South Side of Chicago. Then two years in a liberal arts school within an Amish community near Cleveland. After that, I taught for six years in a rural farm community in the Bible belt. And the rest of my life in Cincinnati.

I give this list as a means to personally observe that there is not one America, and there never has been. Personally, I hope there never will be. I have learned and grown from all these places. What would I be, if I had known only one place, one culture, one way of life? I am rich. Never mind the money, I am rich.

Cincinnati is as black as it is white, and of course, vice versa. In the southwestern corner of Ohio, Cincinnati has accurately been called the nation's northern-most southern city and its southern-most northern city. Cincinnati was one of America's largest cities in the time of the Civil War. As with all the states formed from the Northwest Territory, Ohio was a free state. Ohio was a free state, so of course was Cincinnati. But it lies on the Ohio river. On the other side of that rive was Kentucky, one of the earliest slave states. But Kentucky did not secede, and Union troops were stationed on both sides of the river during the war.

All this to say, Cincinnati was quite familiar with slavery from both sides. Due to various federal law and Supreme Court rulings, slaves present in the free city of Cincinnati, Ohio, were still slaves. They mingled with free blacks from Cincinnati. I can read and study forever, and I don't think I'll ever get my head around that.

It is in Cincinnati that Harriette Beecher Stowe lived, and became informed about the scourge of slavery. Originally from the East, where slavery had very nearly fully died of neglect, she found that in Cincinnati slavery was still commonplace. She didn't have to read about inequality, she walked amongst it. She saw a slave auction in Kentucky. She debated with slave owners. Imagine this: Slavery had been practiced (and still is, in many places) since the beginning of man's time on earth, and in almost every land. The white slavery of the Barbary coast was not a distant memory to her. I ask you to imagine. Imagine what the numerous debates might have been like, between slave owner and abolitionist. It is a one-sided argument today. Not so much, then.

Harriette had to sort out, in her own mind, what the issues really came down to. And then she had to write the most influential book of the nineteenth century, carefully distilling her observations. We think of Uncle Tom's

Cabin today as something of a no-brainer. That was not the case, over 150 years ago. The civil war had been neither perceived nor conceived. An entire country tried to find a way around it. Various means were tried, none succeeded.

There was no deliberate purpose in my finding and reading these three books. I've always been curious about nineteenth century America, and I've always preferred reading the direct word of a person or people, rather than read someone else's interpretation of them. These three people lived very different lives, as we still do today. Somewhere, in and amongst their accounts, the story of their lives and who they are; somewhere in there, we can also learn about ourselves.

We were never one people, and probably never will be. I think this final passage says a lot. Agree, disagree, but based on the various places I've lived in my life, a lot of what Tourgee said over150 years ago, is true today.

17--ALBION

The ostracism of Republicans in business became a tenant of the Democratic Party in the South. It was proclaimed in the political canvass, and individual Democrats were not infrequently denounced for giving patronage to radicals, and for associating in public places with republican leaders. To the northern man, this ostracism on account of political affiliation seems not only absurd, but reprehensible in the greatest degree. The Southerners did not lack the intelligence to see that it could not be justified, consequently they either denied it as a fact, or offered a false explanation.

They were guilty of the greatest social offense known in these slave holding communities; they had affiliated with negroes, had fallen into the cast of pariahs.

Mr. dibble, in his very valuable pamphlet, offers the best explanation of this feeling that has ever been attempted. He says:--

"In order that we may comprehend the disposition of the southerners towards the blacks, let me use an illustration: men do not hate dogs; On the contrary, there exists a strong friendship between master and brute. But if a dog attempts to get upon a man's table, and it persists in his objectionable course, he is apt to be shot for his trouble, and we approve the killing. The southerners did not hate the negroes; On the contrary, there existed between the old slaveholding class and the blacks very kindly relations--far more so than existed between the races in the north. But the average southerner looked upon the blacks at all times and in all respects as inferior beings. They were entitled to be treated kindly, and to be protected in their sphere; but they must not attempt to pass beyond it. Taught by the laws of caste to look upon himself and his class as alone entitled to exercise the prerogatives of citizenship, he resented the disposition of the black man to claim his franchise about in the same spirit in which a man will shoot a dog which has climbed upon the table and will not [get] down."

Mr. Hogan, in the international review for February, 1880, justly measures the force of this feeling when he says:--

"If the negro in the future votes the democratic ticket he will be safe…. If he persists and still being a republican, and boldly calling himself a citizen, no amount of peaceful professions or kindly consideration will save him from being pushed aside by men who indignantly deny him to be their political equal. A leader among the extreme Democrats of the state, general Martin Gary, typifies this latest sentiment of hostility to the negro in the following words: 'the north does not know what it asks of us. No laws or regulations can overcome instinct allied to public opinion. God never made the two races to unite on any ground of equality, and they never will. The white man is the negro's superior, and as such he must remain. The negro cannot be made my social or political equal by any of your laws, and I will never acknowledge him as such!"

The strong individualism which marked the northern colonist, *and which was ever at war with the puritanism which was its own parent,* was almost entirely lacking in the southern colonies. The bulk of the land in these was absorbed by vast holdings, and the larger portion of the laboring classes consisted of those who had been gathered from the peasant classes of the old world, and induced to emigrate only to hold the same relations toward the lordly proprietors in the new; or else they were imported refuse of the prisons and alms houses of England. The commonality of the north, whether of English or Dutch extraction, came hither of their own free will and accord from the old world, either to escape oppression which weighed heavily upon them there, or to lift themselves above the stations which they had previously occupied. They were the best, bravest and most enterprising of their respective classes--those who rebelled had untoward fortune, and determined to improve their fate by the exercise of energy, thrift, and fortitude in the western Wilds. The laborers of the South were either ignorant and mercenary emigres, who were seduced by the promise of greater wages put forth by the proprietors, or those unfortunates who chose exile rather than starvation or transportation [to penal colonies] rather than the prison or the gallows; for it must be remembered that in those days the theft of a few shillings was a capital offense. To put it in a word, the colonists of the north came impelled by the spur of their own conviction; those of the South came on account of extraneous persuasion or compulsion. The former came; The latter were brought.

This difference is clearly perceptible in the governments which were organized after the revolution, and which became component parts of the union. In the one section the rights of the many were most carefully guarded; In the other the rights and privileges of the few were accorded the special protection. The Township system, that perfect crystallization of the primeval democratic idea, with its open town meetings and untrammeled discussion of all matters, both great and small, affecting the interest of the municipality, became, as it were, the unit around which the states of the north were builded. All the institutions which grew out of it were calculated to encourage individuality and personal independence. The north became, therefore, emphatically a nation of free men and equals. Public education flourished as a part of the statal economy, and the idea came universally to prevail that the government was indeed "of the people, by the people, and for the people." Suffrage soon became almost unrestricted; no qualifications beyond that of citizenship was required to make one eligible to any official position; almost all officers were elected by the body of the people; Labor was accounted reputable, and the successful farmer or mechanic found no obstacle in the way of his social or political aspiration; and the humblest pupil of the town meeting found every door yielding readily to his industry and perseverance until even the bronze gates of the capital opened to receive him as a national lawmaker.

At the South all this was reversed. The county was the lowest automatic governmental unit. Authority flowed from the center toward the circumference. The great body of the officers were appointed instead of being elective. The judiciary, the magistracy, the financial officers of the counties, in almost all these states, were selected by the executive or by the dominant party in the legislature. There were no smaller municipal subdivisions than the county. There is no such *witenagemote* as the town meeting, in which the poorest and humblest might have his unrestricted say--might advocate his own theory as to the public weal. Suffrage was restricted in most states to the land owner; only the possessor of an estate of freehold was eligible to official position, to the magistracy, or to service upon the grand and Petit juries; the opening of a public road, the building of a bridge, or any matter of purely local interest, no matter how trivial, could be determined upon only by the county court or some similar tribunal. There was no subdivision of the Commonwealth into self regulating municipalities where the suffragen enacted for himself without the intervention of a representative. As a consequence, the people grew accustomed to being governed instead of governing themselves. Democratic progress was so slow that the impatient student of its past is apt to deny that any was made. Popular education never obtained a firm foothold there as a part of the governmental machinery. As a result, the masses were ignorant and poor; The few, arrogant and rich. The results are well epitomized in Massachusetts and North Carolina.

In the former, slavery was abolished by the growth and eradicating forces of individual liberty; in the latter it was only uprooted as a result of war. In the former, less than four in every hundred of the native white adult citizens are unable to read and write; In the latter, there are 28 out of every hundred of the native whites who cannot read the ballots which they cast. In the former the average wealth per capita is $1250; in the latter, it is $300.

With these governmental differences came also slavery, and added its blighting power to the disabilities which weighed upon the already handicapped masses of the South. The slave holder was also the squirearch and the legislator. Materially, morally, politically and intellectually, the laborer was the dependent and follower of the landlord. Thus it resulted that a minority ruled the South and arrogated to itself the rights, privileges and importance of the whole. The few snubbed and suppressed the many. "The South" came to mean only this dominant minority. Upon all subjects touching their own privileges, this minority--the oligarchy of the South-- was practically unanimous. Against anything which tended to lessen their power they stood as one man. Against a free suffrage and public education they fought long and fiercely. Against free labor free thought and free speech they stood as a wall of fire which none might overlap. *Behind this bulwark, slavery grew strong, malignant, and intolerant of opposition or difference.*

This same people, ignorant and hostile, or arrogant and intolerant, exasperated by defeat and humiliated by poverty, hating the north as an ancient enemy and its institutions as a source of social, moral and political corruption, and degeneracy, constitute the South of today. The ruling class is as arrogant, the poor as abject as ever; for there has been nothing to change their relations or characteristics for the better. To these attributes are added the exasperation and humiliation resulting from the enfranchisement and political exaltation of the negro. To the former master this seemed an insult; to the poor white a threat. To the former it meant a loss of his possessions; to the latter the political coordination of his sole inferior.

From such mental and political conditions came the intolerance which the northern mind finds it so hard to understand. It was in a soil thus prepared that Ku Kluxism struck its roots wide and deep, flourishing as no exotic could, with a strong, vigorous growth of an indigenous stock.

So the mere fact of emancipation would not have stirred up any great hostility against the blacks if they had still remained in some inferior and servile relation, subject to the government direction and control of the whites, their old masters. It was the attempt to make them political equals of the whites which exasperated the latter, because of an implied degradation by being put on the same plane with natural inferiors.

When the southern man says that he has the kindest feeling to the negro in his place, he means in the place for which, according to the southerners notions, nature designed him. His northern listener thinks he means simply a laborer or hired servant, and is struck with his justice, liberality, and reasonableness. When the old master says that he is willing that the nigger should have all his rights, his simple hearted northern listener thinks he means the right to exercise all his political privileges. Not at all. He only means that he should have the wages he earns and be protected in person and property. This he is willing to accord him as a fair thing, which the white race are bound in honor to secure him, so long as he does not interfere with their privileges and seek to share the governing and controlling power. As a mere servitor, he regards the negro kindly; as a political integer [i.e. political equal], he looks upon him with other unappeasable hostility.

Two bits of testimony bring us food for thought--the one is a petition for national aid and the other is a protest against it. Doctor Sears, the learned, patriotic, and philanthropic agent of the Peabody fund, petitions for proceeds of the sales of public lands to be devoted to curing southern ignorance. The New Orleans Picayune, in commenting on this, declares: "The masses of the southern people do not desire school help from the federal government in any form."

But the nation, it must never be forgotten, is responsible for the creation of the massive ignorance by the protection and encouragement which it extended to slavery, and therefore has a duty in the matter which ought not to be shirked.

If this volume shall in any manner tend to aid in the performance of this duty, in directing and stimulating a thought and inquiry and thereby solving the great Riddle which has been put before this generation, the author will feel that the severe experience on which it is based was by no means a fool's errand.

That it will do so he thoroughly believes, and he looks forward to a time when North and South alike shall thank him for the bitter but wholesome truths which he has laid before them for consideration.

A bout the author:
  Chip Kussmaul taught science in public schools for six years at the beginning of his career. Wanting to examine other opportunities, he became an architectural woodworker. Besides commercial work, Chip restored a number of Victorian homes, in a period appropriate manner. He and his wife Jan have lived for many years in one such home, an 1880s Italianate.

  While his career doesn't indicate it, Chip majored in English in college. In retirement, there is time to both read and write.

  The 19th century fascinates Chip. It was one of the most rapidly transitioning centuries in human history. The age of enlightenment was forcing slavery to a close, while the industrial revolution, for better and worse, rapidly changed how people lived.

When he is not writing under his real name, Chip writes under his pseudonym, The Radical Individualist. Much of his work can be found at his Substack site, IndividualistsUnite.Substack.com

IndividualistsUnite.com

IndividualistsUnite.Substack.com